AND GRACE WILL
LEAD US HOME

AND GRACE WILL LEAD US HOME

The Joy of Returning

Frank James Unger

To order additional copies of this book, contact:
Xlibris
1-888-795-4274
www.Xlibris.com
Orders@Xlibris.com
802607

This book is dedicated to
Jennie Brewster,
the Mother of my wife.

PROLOGUE

Ludwig van Beethoven (1770-1827) was a composer of musical masterpieces in spite of deafness that increased with his age. The ingenious Viennese composer then began to carry blank booklets for his acquaintances. A visitor wrote down a question to which Beethoven responded verbally. Often, he used the pocket-sized booklets for shopping lists and sketches for compositions.

In humble reverence, I now borrow from Beethoven, although I'm not deaf and I've slightly altered his format.

In my case, my readers don't write questions. But, like Beethoven, the author does all the talking. He called his efforts *Conversation Books.* And I do the same. In my book, the role of writer is equally as intimate and functional as Beethoven's. There is no deceit on these pages nor was there any on his.

In short, I'll be talking about our cross-country relocation in, *"Grace Will Lead Me Home."* You'll either like the story or you won't, in the same way you either like Beethoven or you don't. In essence, I'll be applying words from his 139 books but avoiding even a single note from his 9 symphonies.

So if you're in the mood for a *music* fix, sorry. I can't oblige. But a *word* fix? Well, Ludwig and I will try our best to entertain you.

I love all of you, especially for reading this.

Thank you, *The Author*

FOREWORD

Some authors know at the start exactly how their book will end. For others, the answer doesn't appear until later in the story. And for another group, they don't have even a clue at the beginning.

This author is in the latter group. Not a clue how it's going to end. Because it's an ongoing tale that begins with the start of a journey. And not even the writer knows where that'll conclude.

So in the role of reader, you'll encounter a lot of uncertainty. You'll be asked to demonstrate patience with both the author and the plot and to accept the outcome, whatever it might be.

Maybe you'll sense the end is near. And maybe not. You might be as surprised as the writer to discover what decisions he and his family make when they reach their destination.

My wife Ginny and I along with our seven children, have never worried about having enough for our happiness and security. Rather, we believe that every obstacle is an opportunity and we live for the moment rather than the past or the future. Perhaps our mantra will help us reach our goal.

So walk with us. But read carefully, because on the printed lines may be a tutorial on how to survive a long-distance move when you're 80+ years old. But more important, in-between those lines, are instructions on how to simply survive your 80's.

Through it all, you can help disprove the theory that, "You can't go home again."

CHAPTER ONE

The Beginning

"We're too old to make a move right now."

"But then again, maybe we're not!"

Though the opening conversation smacked of conflict, Ginny and I agreed to engage the most difficult of all the challenges we faced over 63 years of marriage. This one, however, was different, because our ages didn't allow us to demonstrate the mindfulness of our past nor the time to recover from a failed undertaking.

Friends warned of the pitfalls in returning home again, miming Thomas Wolfe's fatalistic phrase, "You can't go home again." But we were still bold, willing, and able enough to spend our final breaths back with our seven children. We had missed them for almost 20 years of life in Florida. But we were also fatigued by the burgeoning mobs of tourists and snowbirds that crowded the once secluded place known boldly as *paradise.*

And so our arduous journey began . . . two octogenarians inspired by the love of their children and eager to make a change in their own lifestyle, though friends and naysayers said it couldn't and shouldn't be done. "You're too old for stuff like that." "Do you really think your kids are worth it?" "You know the weather in St. Louis is gonna be rough after these nice winters in Florida?"

Negative comments like those weren't exactly encouraging words. But we were determined to prove the skeptics wrong.

First on a lengthy to-do list was the job of getting a realtor to represent us in the sale of our house. It wouldn't be difficult to sell and our agent was optimistic.

Pictures were taken, the place spruced up inside and out, and the "For Sale" sign planted in the center of the front lawn. That was the easy part. Selling the 20-year old house, however, was a bit more complicated.

Three months passed slowly and we were forced to make the second important decision . . . to leave an empty house or move *after* the sale. We chose the former and decided to head north, schlepping far too much furniture and an abundance of keepsakes to last for generations. There was a memory tucked into every available space in each and every one of the 180 cardboard packing boxes.

But before all that, from the very start on the day after Christmas, Ginny and I agreed on almost every element of the move. It was her idea that the void of leaving our children was great enough to draw us back to the Midwest and to sacrifice our near-perfect leisure life on the Southwest coast of Florida.

In this early stage, even I was unusually agreeable, not posing a single objection to her desire to return. That fact, in itself, was the key to the success of the move. If we would've disagreed over every little detail, we wouldn't have made it out of the starting gate. In fact, we never could have survived the multiple challenges and decisions we faced over the first weeks.

Our policy was to cultivate acceptance. We worked hard to support the ideas of each other through a basal orientation of the moving experience. And that wasn't easy. *Moving*, the act of *relocating* has been deemed the second most stressful experience in life, second only to the loss of a loved one. Accepting or rejecting that truth might just determine success or failure. Once we accepted *acceptance*, then, we'd be prepared to accept our frailties, the greatest being the habit of changing our minds, frequently and without control.

I've heard it said that in the mind of the expert, there are few possibilities, but in the mind of the beginner, there are *infinite* possibilities. So we actually benefited from being *beginners,* because we had so many choices on every call we made, from the most significant to the very smallest. But it wasn't easy to make so many quick decisions. Our biggest enemy was fear, fear of defeat; and even though we were of average intelligence, several times we feared we'd crack under the pressure.

And then we learned about teachers and instructors of *meditation* who urged us to embrace the art of *equanimity.* The word itself scared us, because we didn't even know what it meant. Quickly, though, we learned its power and we soon benefited from the wisdom to be "mentally calm, to maintain our composure, and to encounter both good and bad with equal acceptance." That's what equanimity is all about.

So instead of facing every challenge and decision as an obstacle, we embraced it as an opportunity. For it could help us learn and grow smarter in spite of our age. Oh, it took a while to see that materialize. It was much easier to use our age as an excuse, a liability that dragged us down and sapped the stamina from our minds and bodies. But we couldn't let ourselves weaken and whine as we succumbed to pity and/or praise for our actions, however they might be judged.

So the moments of weakness became exercises in strength. We leaned on each other more and more. We did simple things like walking the shoreline of a nearby beach, sometimes holding hands and other times walking in opposite directions to enjoy the comfort of private meditation. Sure, it felt better to hold, to hug tightly, to kiss, and to allow gentle waves to cement our feet to the warmth of soft sand. We learned that having fun together greatly lowered the pressure of our blood and allowed the beauty of intimate relaxation, difficult as it was.

Who wouldn't rather enjoy ageless love rather than surrender to the weaknesses of self-pity and despair. But we needed a sturdy companion to reduce our anxieties and to release our worries.

If you've ever been there, you know how worries can destroy enthusiasm and drain energy from mind and body. Oh, we were learning fast, all right, enough to fill sleepless nights with thoughts and words of wisdom. But not before we discovered how self-defeating sleep deprivation can be.

An early, vital step was to sign a contract with a moving company, one with a good reputation and the solvency of many years in business. In the end, we made the decision based mostly on the sales rep that came to our house, surveyed our belongings and provided a quick estimate. The only talent that mattered more than the expertise of that sales rep was his/her personality. The bottom line, of course, was trust.

We applied simple methods of measuring that important quality. First and foremost was credibility based on instinct, in short, feelings from the gut! If a person had all the answers but he/she appeared uncertain or untrustworthy, no sale. Indeed, the professionalism of the sales rep was a big factor, as were appearance, candor, communication skills and a kindly attitude. That's what it took to be in the running.

But most important, the final call came down to the person we liked the most. So it was a *human* thing that helped us choose a person we felt comfortable in dealing with. When that was done, we made our selection of a mover in just one week.

As in most of our early choices, we followed our instincts. After all, we reasoned, we needed people who could help our cause rather than hinder it, individuals with positive attitudes to relieve our anxiety and to reduce our causes for concern.

There were times when *prioritizing* was the issue, like, which item was most deserving of immediate attention? But that could lead to confusion and unsettled nerves. I mean, we couldn't do everything at once. So we had to learn by doing, moving down the chart of services based on which would lift the greatest burden from our shoulders at the time. And people within those services must have positive attitudes.

Here's an example: by telephone, I switched our Supplemental Health Insurance services from the State of Florida to Missouri. I had been expecting a real hassle, similar to the ones I encountered at the Missouri Division of Motor Vehicles to secure new license plates for our two vehicles. It took me four separate visits to those offices before I actually received my plates.

But the people for *Healthcare* had a different approach: kindness, good wishes, friendliness and knowledge were all demonstrated with confidence and cordiality. Not only did that make for greater efficiency, but it also helped to work with a supplier who was more carefree and enjoyable.

Accomplishing things, scratching them from our list of *things to do,* had actually become a discipline, one that led to a notion of well-being. It helped us develop better attitudes of patience with one another. If we were over-tired and overloaded physically, we learned that our partner probably felt the same. Unselfishness was a key. We grew to a level at which we were more inclined to help one another rather than dwelling on our own discomfort.

We thus grew psychically as well as physically. Compassion, empathy and love became close friends, strengthened and enhanced by genuine caring.

CHAPTER TWO

Moving Forward

It was the style and habit of our realtor to "show" the house on Sunday afternoons. The technique had led to many successful sales over many years so the pattern was applied to our house. Only one obstacle made it more difficult for us. Her name was "Lilly," a large white *Ragdoll* cat. She was charged to pay a price along with the rest of us as she, too, was inconvenienced every Sunday.

To facilitate the realtor's need to sell the house, we promised to make it available for Sunday showings between the hours of 1:00pm and 3:00, the designated time for the "Open House" in Southwest Florida. So every Sunday at about 12:45, Ginny and I hunted down an elusive *Lilly* and as gently as possible inserted her into a "cat carrier."

Now, with most carriers, the cat happily entered from one open end and quickly settled down. But Lilly didn't take kindly to that setup and had to be forcibly *lowered* down into the top of the container, the entire action orchestrated by hissing and howling. The sound made heads turn when/if we carried her into public places. It gave the impression that she was grossly mistreated. The silly expressions on her face drew common scowls.

That problem with Lilly notwithstanding, the routine got a little old after the first three Sundays. Lilly was tiring of it and Ginny and I also had other things we'd rather be doing on Sunday afternoon. But that was not to be, at least not while we remained in our unsold home.

So the habit (the rite of Sunday) consisted of us going to early Sunday Mass, then taking a short break followed by a timely departure from the house at 12:45, leaving it in the hands of the realtor. At first, Lilly didn't appreciate any of that, but she soon accepted the routine. It was up to Ginny and me to figure out how to entertain her for up to two hours in the car.

She was the sensitive kind of feline who wanted to escape from her home but if she ever got outside would panic, possibly even die, if she was thrust into the outside. So we had to get her out of the house during visits by potential buyers thereby demonstrating our concern for her safety if she ever got out. Actually, chances are that she never really *wanted* to escape but was cunning enough to dupe us into the fear of that happening.

Generally, to pass the time of day, we drove around in circles, starting at a nearby Wal-Mart, sometimes enjoying an early breakfast or a later lunch at the Sunflower Café, and returning after two hours of extreme gas consumption and more extreme heat and discomfort in the car. But even after wasting time like that, the routine did nothing to help sell the house.

We were soon faced with an unpleasant option: against our better judgment, we were forced to move north while the house remained for sale but void of furnishings. We would have to take everything with us (including two cars) and pray our hardest for a series of complex plans to fall into place in perfect harmony.

Some realtors preferred selling an *empty* house while the majority preferred selling one that remained occupied and furnished.

A pause in the excitement is in order. I'm going to again explain the purpose of this entire debacle called *A Moving Experience*. I said that the reason to move back to St. Louis from south Florida was to spend more time with our seven children. So if that was the reason for putting ourselves through the chicanery of the moment, a quick review of the Unger's *Magnificent Seven* is in order.

The first-born son was Dan, a cyber-security manager today; then came John one year later. From birth, John was seriously autistic, lacking communication and institutionalized from the age of 6. He continues to reside in a facility near St. Louis.

The third-born was Joseph, a resident of California where he seeks to create, record and perform his original music; next, Mary, the only girl in the lot who is a happily-married Mom "mothering" two wonderful boys; next in line was another son, David, who is a computer programmer who lives with his wife and daughter in St. Louis. Then there's Thomas, married, living in Manhattan and the father of a 17-year-old daughter who thrives in the exciting environment. For a living, Tom works with neon as an artist.

The last of our children was Frank, a proud dad of twins, Nora and Zachary, and husband to a notable marine biologist, Robin. Frank leads his family as a stay-at-home dad and works as a film animator of movies. His claim to fame was to be a member of the team of artists who won an Oscar for its work with Director Ang Lee on the 2012 Drama/Fantasy film, *Life of Pie*.

That's it. At last count, the total was seven. And Ginny and I are proud of each of them. Now, even though only Dan, John, and David live in St. Louis, we knew we'd see more of the others who found traveling to St. Louis a lot easier than getting to Florida. So our motivation for moving back to the Midwest was, indeed, justified.

Back to our storyline. As the day of the move (March 8th), drew closer and the sale of the house looked more like a dim light fading behind us, we began to wonder if we misread God's message to "pull up stakes." Perhaps He was actually advising us to, "Stay put." So that slight doubt caused some hesitation on our part.

No, it didn't help our spirits to follow the weatherman, either. While it was perfectly beautiful in Ft. Myers, the St. Louis area was fighting off one of the worst winters in history: strong winds, tons of snow, and miserable driving conditions. It certainly would have caused *anyone* to reconsider a plan as absurd as ours.

And so we did. But it was too late. We had placed deposits on every stage of the move to St. Louis: the mover, the auto transport company, the apartment we "saved" as it waited for an occupant, and the many other services in our new area of habitation. In effect, we were growing deeper and deeper into doubt as well as into debt, not just in the task at hand, but financially as well.

Okay, so here's a quick rundown of the plans and deadlines we faced. March 6th was the day the movers had targeted to begin the *packing* stage. All packing of all materials from inside the house was to be labeled and packed into boxes and completed on that single day.

March 7th, then, was designated as *loading* day, the day the van arrived and the material was placed inside. It was also the day the auto carrier began hauling the two cars. But the day was also critical to secure the services of a neighbor/friend who took us to a local Hotel because the house was made empty and we had nowhere to sleep for that one last night. How could all that possibly happen at the same time?

March 8th was D-day, so to speak, the day we were scheduled to physically depart the area and fly to St. Louis with Lilli tagging along in her carry-on traveling case. We received a wakeup call from the hotel front desk at 5:00am and a taxicab picked us up at the front entrance. We departed at exactly 6:00am: two humans, one cat, four suitcases and lots of prayers. We made comparisons to the early American pioneers who set out for the Wild West in much the same manner. The only difference was the Conestoga wagons they used for transport over one month instead of two hours on a jet.

Each portion of our *wagon train* was scheduled to arrive at precisely the same time, on Saturday morning, the 9th of March. Of course, Ginny and I did not even plan on any sleep over those last four nights. Our nerves were frozen in place. We scarcely spoke to one another. And throughout the period, my *sciatica* attacked with a fury of pain in my left leg. (It would choose inappropriate times like that to let us all know that it had not cured itself but was sticking around to cause as much additional damage as possible.)

But surprises were in order. God was listening. And our faith once again saved us. As we arrived at our apartment on the morning of the 9th of March, we were forced to slow down . . . to make room for the mover's 62-foot vehicle and the auto transport vehicle that carried our cars. There they were, ahead of us, same minute, same day, waiting for us in our apartment driveway.

We all made it together safely. The stress drained quickly from our bodies, Lilli panted to be released from her cage, and there was a tear or two from the exhausted family leaders.

Just when our faith was waning, the Good Lord rescued us. He had saved His best for last! My good friend, Tom, always claims that the Almighty is a show-off, generally waiting until things look near hopeless to prove His might and majesty with a dramatic flourish. He did it well this time around.

CHAPTER THREE

Still Another Challenge

It was a time for reflection. We all arrived safely and on time, so what? It was supposed to be that way. *No surprises* are what we had been promised. But what about the *other* issues that were indeed the worst kind, the kind one never expects. What about those?

Flashback! After the moving truck pulled away from the curb in front of our Ft. Myers house, we noticed mountains of boxes and furniture that remained in the garage and/or on the driveway. When we inquired about those *forgotten* pieces, the reply from the head driver was something like, "Oh, we ran out of space. Your sales rep reported on the number of pieces to be hauled but his number was off from the number we actually packed, off by about *80 boxes more* than the estimate!

"Bottom line here is that we can't fit all your stuff on one truck. We'll send another back in a couple of days to pick up the remainder. If we're lucky, we might even get the two trucks up there around the same time!"

What? We were startled by all the things that were missing from the first truck when the movers unloaded at our new residence in St. Louis. We were speechless . . . "Speechless in St. Louis." The second truck arrived over a week later, with a backlog of materials that we faced *after* the first truck was long gone.

That simple clerical error dragged everything down, including our spirits and attitudes. The delay in getting that second truck of furniture and personal belongings was the straw that broke the camels back.

But we recovered. Because we had been *trained* to recover, to bounce back from disappointments that went with the territory. Here we were, smug and over-confident about making all the right choices, like the first big one about the selection of the moving company. We were so far off on that one that it was pathetic.

On reflection, the largest portion of our learning came from our mistakes. The problem was that we had no plans to ever move again, especially at our age. So the learning we accumulated would not be of any use unless we reduced the number of years we had left on the planet. And we were not in favor of that.

It boiled down to evaluating our biggest blunders. The first was our selection of the mover. And the biggest was in calculating the stuff we had elected to take. We grossly underestimated the comparative sizes of the two dwellings. We thought we had ourselves covered, but we weakened in our estimate of what we *wanted* to take versus what we *could* take.

In the end, it wouldn't take as much to live in St. Louis in our older years as it took in the prior years with seven kids and a house. Our hobbies had been reduced due to age. The need for furniture had fallen because we weren't going to entertain as much. And lastly, we lived a lifestyle that required less home cooking and more restaurant foods. Hence, the huge load of kitchen supplies was out of line with what we actually needed.

And then, of course, there was the massive collection of memorabilia, from my family as well as Ginny's. Dozens, *hundreds* of pieces ranging all the way back to marriage keepsakes from both families. We thought we had agreeably covered all that in our private planning conferences, but we had barely scratched the surface.

I could double the pages of this book if I surrendered a list of the exact number of things we carried with us that we'll never use again, mostly from the kitchen but also many items from dressers and closets and cedar chests and dish cabinets and armoires and wardrobes.

We'll never use those pieces of memorabilia, never. We'll probably never even *see* them from underneath the mountains of packing paper. And there aren't many people eager to take over ownership of such old treasures.

So we arrived in St. Louis significantly behind our schedule, the one that was made to be broken. It was *then* that we ran into the *really* serious delays, beginning with four separate trips to the Missouri Department of Revenue, Motor Vehicle Bureau, to purchase new license plates. (I mentioned that before but it deserves a reminder.) Of course, each of those trips was caused by our lacking some crucial piece of information, which I won't go into because I trust everyone has been there.

But that didn't close the license saga. Even after I had the plates in hand, I learned that although in Florida, only one plate is required, in Missouri, another is required on the *front* bumper. So, for each of two vehicles, a license plate *frame* had to be ordered and attached to the front. Each of those front frames cost $75.00! So one trip didn't do it. *Three* trips to the dealership for each one finally got things right.

We hadn't thought about all the other business needs: auto and home insurance, health insurance for Medicare and supplemental, new medical and dental searches for suitable local services, and changes of address for all credit cards, banks, and financial institutions.

Was it all worth it? Well, it'll take awhile to determine. For the moment, we greatly appreciate frequently mixing with our children and grandchildren. But we're far from settled. And we know that there are a few surprises to come. And they may not be good ones.

We've accumulated uncountable numbers of tall stacks of brown cardboard boxes, piled neatly in our one-car garage. They stand from the floor to the ceiling and go ten deep from front to back. Needless to say, it's difficult for a human body to enter and exit a vehicle.

Somebody with the moving company had explained early on (prior to our signing the contract) that the mover would pick up the boxes when the job was finished. But we learned that a charge for the pickup of the 180 boxes was to be $320.00, not an insignificant amount.

So we went on a search for other sources of box pickup and disposal, places like Goodwill Industries, Church organizations, etc. To date, the boxes still remain in our garage; but compared to other aggravations, it's a minor hassle . . . unless we're forced to *see them*!

On the plus side, one of the great features of our apartment is that it has a full basement. Now, that can be a curse rather than a blessing. Because the temptation is to store everything where no one can see it. That, in itself, can create quite a mess. It's mostly clothing and fabric remnants and patterns from Ginny's hobby of sewing. Those items alone fill over twenty boxes. Blend them with errant kitchen utensils and recipe books and you have what's known as a basement graveyard.

In a moment of complete honesty, I admit that both Ginny and I get a little depressed from time to time. We work so hard to make a noticeable difference each and every day, and yet, sometimes, it's hard to tell. Frequent visits from the kids serve as a distraction, a pleasant pause to enjoy the fruits of our labors.

Very honestly, our sons, daughter-in-law, and granddaughter have contributed more than we would ever expect with frequent visits, sleeves rolled up, ready to work hard to help us. One by one, they tear boxes apart, sorting the contents, disposing of trash. From time to time, when needed, they even bring food, purchase dinners, run errands and provide needed moral support. They are beyond anything we imagined, because they have their own lives and still find time to help us. If it was not for those efforts, we never could make even mild inroads. Their closeness and loving encouragement are also beyond reproach. Hugs and kisses and many, many "I love you's" keep us going. Such gestures ring true forever.

After almost twenty years of living 1,500 miles apart, with only infrequent Holiday visits, we cannot believe that we're merely saying "goodnight" at the end of a day, instead of "goodbye" to our children. That has been unusually great! "No pain, no gain!" It's the motto heard around our household. We all suffered the *pain* together and now we're enjoying the *gain* together.

I'm pleased to mention, too, that our joy in visiting John more frequently is immense. Right now, his future is as clouded as his mind and no one can chart his life expectancy. Ginny and I never thought he would outlive us and now it appears as though he might as he reaches his 62nd birthday.

We pray that God will eventually take him to His breast, hold him fondly in His arms, and draw his human life to a quiet close. So we cherish this extra time that we've been given to spend with him. It's part of a special bonus that came with the loving idea to return to St. Louis. That idea has now mushroomed into a force to reckon with, guided by patience, peace, love and gratitude.

John could never travel to Fort Myers on public transportation to visit his mom and dad. The distance and the risk of adverse behavior were far too great. But now, we've brought our love to him, without risk but with parental caring and sharing. The added comfort has been overwhelming.

CHAPTER FOUR

Reflection . . . Again!

Well, since I appear to have everything worked out, I'm ready to spring a surprise that'll open me to great criticism . . . and worse!

In spite of everything you've read so far, written in my hand, I went to bed last night seriously unhappy. Seems like all the bad stuff finally caught up with me, i.e. broken dreams, sleepless nights, allergies, lousy food, and in general, physical and mental misery. All at the same time. Hit me like a ton of bricks. Thankfully, Ginny is not yet stricken. But since she isn't, how am I going to break the news of my discovery to her, without causing an uproar and a serious quake in our relationship.

How about something like, "I've changed my mind about this moving North thing." Or maybe a little softer like, "I'm miserably unhappy here and want to go back to Florida!" No, I think I can be more subtle: "I hate it here and I want to go back!"

I guess I'm so beat-up that I just can't fight it any longer. It's time to surrender. The joy of being near the kids has worn off and I'm thinking selfishly again.

Truthfully, it feels good. Visions of Palm trees. Fresh seafood. Blue waters. Clean air. I must have been crazy to consent to this move. I forgot how heavenly it was there.

In fact, I can provide a noteworthy example of a visual difference between Fort Myers and St. Louis. Trust me now because I'm not fabricating any of this. This is a microcosm of the *ornithology* of the two places. The comparison offers factual evidence of which environment is more attractive to the average human resident as well as to the resident *birds* who have chosen to populate the area.

At our house in a very ubiquitous neighborhood of Fort Myers called *Coconut Creek,* there are flocks of ducks who stop by every morning as well as flocks of *white and black Ibis*, who parade across our lawn every single day, all day long.

And there are other rare guests like the *American Bald Eagle*, many of whom have stood on our lawn and fished in the lake right in front of our eyes, at close range. And a familiar relative of the Eagle known as *Osprey* who visit in great numbers and select small fish as they dive from high in the sky and snatch their prey from the lake.

The *Cormorant* and *Anhinga* and *the Great Blue Heron,* and *Great White Egret*, and the flocks of smaller *Snowy Egrets* are all native to Florida and parts of the Caribbean. Additionally, there are seasonal visitors like the *Wood Stork*, and *White Pelicans* who come all the way from the State of Washington . . . all of them right in our back yard.

The fact is that many of the birds fly over from a bird Sanctuary on Sanibel Island called *Ding Darling* which is on a direct path across the bay to our lake. They come in flocks, circle the lake, fish a little, then head back to their nesting places on Sanibel Island. Also, it's not just the *sightings* of these birds that entertain us . . . it's the *songs* they sing, each one unique to the others.

Truly, our property has been blessed with some of the most beautiful wild birds of Florida, in addition to other seasonal guests who breed there, like the wonderful turtles. And there's one friendly fish who's respectively nicknamed "Jaws." He hangs out near the shoreline and experts have determined from his large dorsal fin that he's one of the common Tilapia who has been stocked in the lake in great abundance.

So when, how is this shocking appraisal revealed to the person I love more dearly than anyone in the world? Why would I risk making her sad? Well, only if my focus is regained and I believe deeply that she'll be better off for it. That's the only way it can be done. And it must be done. She must *want* to move back to Florida!

All the traumatic events had finally taken their toll. It was time to fess up, to return to sanity, to regroup, to move forward instead of backward. If we did things right this time, maybe we could add another ten happy years to our lives. But we'd have to begin in complete harmony, Ginny and me in total agreement. One of us must take the role of advocate. She'll understand.

Her reply was quick and simple . . . "You've completely lost your mind!" (Subtlety was not her strength.) Her initial response wasn't gentle either, signifying a battle not to be easily resolved. I'd have to love and appreciate her more than ever, in spite of her immediate resistance. That, I can deliver!

"How can you say such things . . . 'you want to go back. You hate it here.'"

"Darling, please listen to me. Calm down and give me a chance to explain."

"Explain? Explain what? We've been working on this for over a month now. And you say, "I want to go back?"

"Be reasonable, my dear."

Nothing seemed to help. I pleaded for common sense, over and over again.

"Do you mean to say you're ready to give up on all this, all the positive things we've started? The kids nearby? We're a family again, aren't we?"

"We always were. Just a little geography between us." Ouch! What a mistake. Never should have said that. Keep my mouth shut. Listen only. Don't talk. Keep quiet and take every blow before I speak sensibly.

"What did you say? Did I hear the word 'sensibly?'"

"No, darling. Just thinking out loud."

"I cannot believe you're talking like this. You agreed to do whatever it took to make this work. Now, you're going back on your word . . ."

"Okay," I began, "I'll speak slowly. Listen!"

I explained in soft words and quiet tones. I pointed out that I had nothing to do here. I was bored to death. In Fort Myers, I had beaches, places to spend time thinking, writing, forming ideas, within natural, inspirational backdrops. In St. Louis, all I had was a lousy arch, busy highways, terrible weather . . . and a few boring birds. Yes, boring . . . cardinals, blue jays, blackbirds, robins, etc.

In-between my pleas, Ginny offered little objection, but made up for the absence by shaking her head negatively. She wanted to argue for the sake of it, but I declined to take the bait, continuing to list my general dissatisfaction

"Sweetheart," I said in a hush, "this place is just not for me. It never was and never will be. You know how much I loved Florida, the yard work I used to do . . . twelve months of the year. It was a pastime. It helped to stimulate my creativity. I can't write without that stuff. The landscape here is barren, colorless. The skies are grey not blue. And the pollen. I'm about to die from the pollen, sneezing all day and night.

"In a nutshell . . . it's drab around here. It's absent of color. And the people. They're as drab as the landscape. The deprivation of sunlight makes them this way. They need vitamin A and D for health reasons in addition to making themselves more attractive with a mild tan.

"You know yourself, my dear," I said, speaking ever so softly so as not to antagonize her loaded sensitivities. I counted my blessings that she actually agreed with some of my comments.

"And the food," I said. "Have you noticed all the overweight people around here. It's from all the fatty, greasy food they eat, meatloaf, mashed potatoes, etc. You remember those fresh seafood meals we'd enjoy, at *outdoor* restaurants beside the water. That was food and that was living, *healthy* living, in a quiet, cool breeze with the smell of salty water, island music, and my favorite, Jimmy Buffett. His songs were everywhere."

That mention of *Jimmy Buffett* got to her. She actually laughed at me, trying to be cute, ruffled her hair, shifted in her chair and mimed the words again, like in my face . . . "*Jimmy Buffet?*" That hurt a bit but I was ready to move on to bigger things.

I thought it would help make a point if I mentioned *Manchester Road,* a very busy street in our area and the main thoroughfare for commerce and business. It didn't help at all.

"Can't you see what an ugly road that is, dear, compared to *Gladiolus Drive* in Fort Myers. The name itself tells you something. *Manchester Road* is cluttered with everything obnoxious: crooked telephone poles, dozens of billboards, gaudy advertising. Nothing's managed. No continuity. Gladiolus, on the other hand, has a handsome uniformity befitting its name. There are laws that control the views and the colors. There's an effort to maintain aesthetic qualities."

"Disagree! There's continuity on Manchester."

"The only continuity is that it's all tasteless, dark, and unpleasant. It matches the sky for most of the year." That was all I said, but Ginny refused to give me any points. It was my turn again.

I pinpointed all the driving dangers and hazards along Manchester Road. The stop signs, short turns, mismarked lanes and an overabundance of autos and trucks. But it did nothing to convince her that I had any kind of edge in the traffic category. She got in another dig.

"Speaking of traffic," she said. "How about the snowbirds in Florida at this time of year. You know how frustrated you became driving there from September until like April?"

"Granted," I said quickly, ". . . granted that I get very impatient with those extra people we have to tolerate during the busy season. But it's my fault. If I could be more patient . . . I mean, it's my fault. I could tolerate them again in a minute if I had that beautiful weather."

The discussion went on for over an hour. Neither of us would surrender to the other. Each believed her/his point-of-view was the most accurate and the most appealing. But which of us was winning the battle? I really loved Ginny so much that I didn't want to win any argument. She was frail and helpless and always looked so pitiful and beautiful when we argued like this. I felt sorry for her vulnerability. She reminded me of a little girl being attacked by a bully. So I eased up on her with a more feasible suggestion. It was worth a try.

I proposed this: "As soon as our *for sale* house sells in Fort Myers, as soon as that happens, how about if we become 'snowbirds.' Why couldn't we take the money from the sale and pretend it belonged exclusively to maintaining a lifestyle in Fort Myers? And conversely, use the money we already had in savings before the move up north to maintain our lives in St. Louis.

"Oh, there are a lot of details to be worked out, but I'd bet we could do it. The only real loss would be paying rent for the apartment in St. Louis while we enjoyed winter in Florida. And since we had two cars anyway, why not join the crowd of northerners who formed a caravan that ventured south in the wintertime. Sounds good to me."

At first blush, Ginny accepted the idea. Her only hesitation was in doubting we'd have enough cash to live comfortably in St. Louis in the off-season. We agreed that it would require a lot of detailed speculation and skilled guesswork to prove the economics feasible. But the idea was worth exploring and the subject open. For the time being anyway, I was happy to see Ginny pleased and open to discussion. We both agreed to agree and to at least consider the other's point-of-view before any veto. I would sleep better tonight.

I think it's time that we pause to make comparisons of houses and environments. First, the one we lived in for nearly 20 years in Florida.

Built in 2000, it housed three bedrooms, family room, kitchen, dining room and utility room, with a screened back porch (lanai) along the entire rear of the house. Total footage without porch was 2,600 square feet. Similarly, the apartment we were renting in St. Louis had three bedrooms also with family room, kitchen, dining room, living room and full basement. The rooms in St. Louis were smaller but there was that full basement for storage. Square footage of living area was 1,700. Hence, a comparison indicates less living space in St. Louis.

Now, the difference between the two is not dramatic in measurable square footage, but the lifestyle the house supports is. In Florida, that back porch I mentioned faced a private lake stocked with Tilapia,

Bass, Snook, and not a small amount of very active turtles of all sizes. It also attracts dozens of shore birds, some who remain all year and others who migrate from the colder temperatures in various seasons. The flowery odor from this exterior, the aroma from the flowers and soil and water fills the air with such delight that nowhere in America, is there anything quite like it.

The birds add even more, a colorful and entertaining backdrop to the dense foliage that surrounds the quietude of Florida. All of these natural amenities provide a relaxing ambience that "comes with the territory" and never gets old.

It's completely the opposite at our apartment in St. Louis. Instead of the wide, screened porch, there's a narrow balcony that backs off onto a plot of grass that separates us from the rear entrance of a shopping mall. There *is* some foliage, but small trees provide only spring blooms for several weeks.

And the sounds are not from songbirds, but rather, from plentiful numbers of motored vehicles that wind through the thoroughfares and parking lots. Wildlife sounds are from large Canadian geese and small squirrels that complement the noise. (If this writer appears hostile to one side of the appraisal, that feeling is displayed by his honesty and supported by the facts of these two places.)

CHAPTER FIVE

What's Next?

One step forward, two back. That's the rate at which we progress in our new surroundings. Case in point:

Just a week ago, we received an alarming phone call from John's place of residence. He was attending his daily program (classes with fellow students) and he used force to defend himself against an aggressor. Such events occur frequently in such a place where no one is directly responsible for his/her actions but someone must be held accountable. It's generally the first person who takes physical action and injures another who gets the blame and the second person is then not regarded guilty if he/she is defending himself. Easier said than done when neither party is behaving reasonably because of a mental lapse.

So, the phone just rang again and it was John's school reporting that John "scratched someone." As I heard the message, I responded with a logical, "Someone had better figure out what's provoking John and put an end to this. Somebody could be seriously injured in one of these encounters."

The woman phoning from his school, reasonably replied, "Our psyc department is very concerned about it and is investigating the cause. They will then take steps to separate the two men to make certain it doesn't happen again." I agreed and felt great compassion for both men.

Just as I hung up the phone, Ginny came into the room and explained that a set of two bookcases being delivered from a retailer to us were delivered to the wrong address in our apartment complex. It was an extremely heavy shipment and I was at a loss for knowing exactly what to do to recover the misplaced merchandise. It was on the wrong person's front porch on the second floor.

With credit due to responsible management, our maintenance crew was picking up the boxes and delivering them to our place. That kindness was greatly appreciated but logged as, "just another daily aggravation that reduced fairly good spirits."

The big question now was how to evaluate this accumulation of negative events and make some kind of judgment: was it simply a run of bad luck or a message from the Almighty that this *moving experience* was considerably over our heads.

Perhaps we should take action and save ourselves from further disasters. Or maybe there's nothing we can do to stop such events, save only to run away from our decision and head back to Florida. Up until now, that choice was impossible, impractical, and totally out of the question!

But in order to survive, we'd have to again embrace our "acceptance" theory, i.e., accepting human frailties and joining together to work it all out. Corny to say it, but *teamwork* was the only solution for survival. Assembling the strength and courage of 63 years of marriage, we knew we could do it with the help of God! But our handicap was being 83 and 84 years old? We had some doubts.

Speaking of health: my sciatica is still a painful annoyance and Ginny's aching back is formidable. So we're not in the best shape but we're not in the worst shape either. Good health has been a blessing.

You know, I've talked about this before, it's not simply *accepting* the ups and downs, those uncontrollable forces that limit progress, but the real art is in developing the *discipline* to reflect on good times and to allow those positive thoughts and memories to govern ones life. Again, easier said than done. But it's a reasonable goal.

Believing that strongly motivates us to begin every day with a commitment to be positive. But then the phone rings and it's some insurmountable problem, like an unforeseen auto repair, a bad stomach from a bad meal the night before, maybe another call on John's behavior.

Prayer! Most of the time, it's the immediate place to seek help, the immediate path on which to discover hope, though not always the quickest way to solve a problem. Because sometimes the good Lord works slowly, testing faith and patience before making a decision.

You've heard of the prayer called the "Hail Mary" as it applies to football. It's a last-ditch effort by the losing team to pull out a victory. The odds aren't very good that it'll work, but it's the only chance to win if you're losing. Well, we happen to think that we've already thrown one dozen "Hail Mary's." The most recent is another drop in the price we're asking for our house. Nothing else has worked, so it's worth a try. But the chances are slim that the new price will attract a buyer who hasn't had interest before. So . . . with all the faith we can muster, we've said the prayers, er, thrown the ball into the end zone one more time.

We're convinced that if we can sell that Florida house, we'll have a better attitude about *acceptance*, be more inclined to make all the other pieces of the puzzle fall into place. Perhaps it's just an excuse to remain grumpy, but as the funds are being depleted, we have a growing concern about running out of money. That's a biggie!

In many ways, our separation from the seashore has had its impact. A nice, long walk on a soft, sandy beach always produced a certain magic in meditation, blending the soft sound of the waves with a clear breeze and the splash of a dolphin passing near the shore. Escape! It was a clear and pure *escape* like no other. But to be fair to Missouri, here's yet another color to add to the palette.

The other day, rather than complaining about the weather, etc., we took to the highway. We drove west on a road called, Wild Horse Creek. It was equally as beautiful a drive as any we'd seen in Florida, with several notable differences. In Florida, the roads were straight and wide with lots of Interstates. On Wild Horse Creek Road, the entire road was narrow and winding, hilly and depleted of traffic. Gentle streams wound around the road with occasional bridges marked, "single lane only."

Both driver and passenger could *hear* the music of fresh water tumbling along clean rocks as it followed every curve across historic paths. This was Lewis and Clark territory and there was no doubt what inspired them to influence the founding of a great city beside the river called Mississippi. We were delighted to find such a peaceful, abundant forest teeming with deer, possum, badger, otter and many less noticeable creatures. It was a small victory on our part to be able to admit that.

But this journey is a travelogue to truth. If we're not honest with ourselves, there's no way we'll make the right decision. So admitting to the beauties of Missouri and St. Louis is not a sign of weakness, it's a sign of our commitment to truth.

For goodness sake, we cannot surrender to the State of Florida and the city of Fort Myers just because we *liked* it more in one place than the other. There must be soluble reasoning, an emotionless evaluation to stay our course.

We're halfway toward a happy solution, but we're not there yet. During that other half, the road grows steeper. So it's going to take investigation, evaluation, deliberation, a lot more than we've done so far. We've already learned the hard way that there's no room for cowards on our train. Because of our age, there's no slowing down when we hit a sharp curve.

In short, we've got to galvanize our abilities, draw them together to excite and energize our ambitions. And that's going to take unlimited creativity, not just by Ginny and me, but by all the members of our family and friends who care about our success in achieving our goals.

All we want from this journey is to be happy. We don't need wealth to achieve that. Nor do we need a life of perfection or a scenario of trouble-free days and nights. We do need one another, though, working in harmony without selfishness or stubbornness. We've got to think of each other first, ourselves last, and God always. It's one of our strongest beliefs. Ourselves last, others first, and God always. No matter how you switch the emphasis, it begins and ends the same.

Earlier, I mentioned what I call "The Basement Graveyard." There is nowhere in the house where the lack of progress is so pronounced and where the desperate need for creativity is so visible. The only saving grace is that we're only forced to see it when we willingly walk down the steps.

I dared to go there this morning and when I returned upstairs, I warned Ginny, "Please," I said, "don't ever venture those stairs without me at your side." She smiled and asked "Why?"

I could only smile back and plead, "Why? Because you have no concept of just how many boxes are still to be opened, unpacked, and recycled into useable contents that we carried here from Florida. My closing remark about *The Graveyard* was simply, "utterly devastating. Leave it alone!"

Maybe if the boxes were all the same size, the challenge would be easier. But some measure 30 inches tall and 18 inches wide; some are 18 inches square; and others are two feet square. The contents are mostly remnants of clothing; but there are surprises in nearly every box, things like forgotten recipe books, my college text books, even hundreds of assorted "thank you" notes, greeting cards, and blank pages of note paper in all sizes and designs.

My quick inventory lists more than 30 packed boxes in the basement and another 30 empty ones remaining in the garage. That's a very large load of many, many boxes, in a wide range of sizes.

So, here's where the *Graveyard* problem is intensified in complexity. There are a few pieces of large furniture down there that really should come up first, if for no other reason than to make more room. They vary in weight and size, things like a cedar chest, a bookcase, a china cabinet, etc. So, such large and heavy items must be carried up and disposed of *first!* It would be emotionally uplifting (pun intended).

But no company wants to go down and get the stuff, primarily because it can endanger the lives of their employees as they carry it to the upstairs. All philanthropic enterprises are hesitant to handle big stuff from a basement because of liability dangers.

We've tried most of the resources that handle such things and so far, only one will touch the stuff. That's a group referred to as *College Hunks.* They provide a quote on their first visit and for that price will haul away all the stuff and legally dispose of it.

Right now, they're all that we have, so we'll be forced to employ them. Our frustration is that we should've known better. We should have left every piece of *The Graveyard* back in Florida. Because it's all junk. We'd never miss a single piece if we dumped it sight unseen into the depths of the Mississippi, although Ginny might have some reservations about such a dramatic decision. All I can say for right now is, stay tuned for new developments as they might arise, (another pun).

CHAPTER SIX

Even More Complexities

There are times when we awaken with no agenda, no plan for what to do with the day. We are as listless as a foundering ship, lost in purpose and direction. It's left us drained and confused. We've been taught that the best approach to regaining sanity is to have a plan every day. But during the course of our move from Midwest to south and back again, we've been so shaken from our roots that we don't know which way to turn, or in which direction our roots were planted in the first place.

A number of years ago, when Dan was about eleven, we were living in Dallas and facing a choice between two houses we wanted to buy. One was a bit nicer than the other but a bit more expensive. We were torn between making a practical decision or one that would cost us more money.

Ginny and I approached Dan, the eldest of the young family of four children. But he was wise beyond his age and generally made sound choices when given the opportunity. So we approached him regarding our dilemma.

"Son, which house do you think we should buy?" we asked him. He thought about it for no more than a minute and replied, "Well, I think you should buy the one you like the most."

His profundity amazed us. Here we were, buried in facts and figures about monthly payments, square footage, size of lot, affordability, and other such cold facts. But Dan had the wisdom to cut through all that and boil it down to purely emotional desire. "Buy the one you like the most."

So we did! And we were pleased with the results and lived happily in that house for five years before I took a job in St. Louis and we were on the move, the second of about thirteen location changes spaced over our 63 years together.

But the lesson Dan taught us was the fact that sometimes, in making horrendously complex decisions, it's smart to throw away the technical jargon and analytical ideas and simply choose what appeals to you the most. If you want to make it work, you can do it . . . with enough desire, ambition, wisdom, and just plain common sense.

Not surprisingly, Dan has now reached the age of 62 and is still making sensible decisions, good choices that have propelled him into a happy and deserving lifestyle and a path of success.

So, for a minute, it's legitimate to apply Dan's eleven-year-old wisdom to our current situation. If Ginny and I were to evaluate all the facts and figures between staying in St. Louis or moving back to Florida, weigh the good versus the bad and make a choice solely based on emotion . . . well, it wouldn't take long to decide to return to Florida. Just pack everything up, unopened boxes and all, and head south to the *Sunshine State*. And on the way, contact a couple of good local realtors in Fort Myers and have them scout out a reasonable place for us to rent, at least for a new start.

What do you think? According to Dan's philosophy and simple wisdom, we should do what we want the most, e.g., returning to beaches, friendly winters, all of that and more could again be ours as we seek only a simple, happy life for the two of us. Let's have a vote on it! Those in favor of leaving all our headaches behind in St. Louis and returning to a place where we were so happy . . . put your hands together!

Those who think we should stay and tough it out so the family can remain physically closer to one another, close your book right now. If you want, put your hands together and applaud!

Hold on for a minute. Think carefully, ponder deeply . . . should we think of the kids first and stay geographically close to them, or should we make things right for ourselves and head back south?

Aha . . . not so easy, huh? Dan's *youngster wisdom* isn't as crystal clear now as it was when he was eleven and the stakes weren't as high. That's because everyone in the family had a whole life ahead of him and her, tons of time to reverse course and start over if they felt they had made a mistake.

But now, for Ginny and me, we're running out of time and must be certain to make the right choice for everybody concerned. So we've got to think this out slowly, with great deliberation, and with a lot of help from that Almighty Person Who brought us all together in the first place. We ask with an open heart . . . please, God, lead us in the right direction for the benefit of our family.

(Pause for a moment of silent prayer.)

If you're at a loss for words, say the following: "Dear God in heaven, please give Ginny and Frank the wisdom, knowledge and unselfishness to make a decision based on their own happiness as well as the joy and happiness of their seven children. Inspire them to open their hearts, to hear your words and to be comforted by your love in this difficult time. In St. Louis or in Fort Myers, bring them the peace they have shared for a lifetime but have lost on this unusual journey.

Amen

Now, hold on a minute. Since we're exploring all the possible avenues of escape, let's consider another one, only 300 miles to the north of St. Louis lies the city of Chicago, the birthplace of Ginny and me. It's not a bad place to live, in spite of big city problems like racial strife, pollution, high taxes and a history of crime and crooked government. Ginny and I continue to love it on twice-a-year jaunts we've made up there every six months.

The amenities of Chicago reprise our childhood. It has the best restaurants in all of America, with an ethnic focus of Italian, Greek, Polish, German, and all the rest. Especially in the downtown area and in local neighborhoods that breed such choices, there are ethnicities that, at the same time, prevent boredom and please the palette.

We celebrated our 62nd wedding anniversary up there last August at our favorite hotel, the Drake. It's an historic place that's built at Oak Street beach and The Outer Drive. One of the most elegant Hotels in all the world, the Drake has hosted the world's finest actors, musicians, world leaders and politicians. Conveniently, The Drake is walking distance to some of the city's best eating-places and entertainment venues along *The Magnificent Mile.*

And downtown Chicago is loaded with an array of places to *live* . . . loft apartments, condo skyscrapers, and elegant homes and apartments. If we lived there, we could still maintain a close relationship with our local family (namely John, Dan and David). The six-hour drive or one-hour flight could assure an adequate amount of visits. Additionally, Ginny has close family in Chicago with male and female cousins galore within the boundaries of the suburbs.

To live there in a downtown condo, choosing the most dramatic change for the last years of our lives, to live there in such a residence might be quite affordable and equally exciting, that is, once we sold the house in Fort Myers. We could actually live without a motor vehicle and rely exclusively on public transportation. And we could even have a beach at our convenience throughout the summer.

Now that's a thought worthy of consideration. But so is the idea of *remaining* in St. Louis and capitalizing on all the wonderful amenities of Chicago, only 300 miles away and easily accessible. At this point, the choice of relocating to Chicago full-time and permanently, merely complicates our current, exasperating dilemma. How and why can I continue to make this *Moving Experience* more intensely unsettled and complex? (I always find a way.)

CHAPTER SEVEN

A New Agenda

A professional Psychoanalyst would define me as "a related individual who is part of a group of people who are completely repressed and causing psychic conflict leading to abnormal mental states of behavior." Is that really what I'm becoming these days? Yes, the entire scenario is far too complex for a simple guy like me to handle, especially with my deep appreciation for my wife's happiness.

Over these past several months, it's no wonder that the two of us have grown apart. It's not like the old days when we were lovingly inseparable. We're more irritable, less compassionate, too busy for love. And it's not really our fault. We don't love each other any less. But we have too much clutter in our minds to demonstrate caring as deeply as we should. Hence, our vulnerability and reaction to common daily problems has been reprehensible.

Within a two-week period, for example, we were unduly aggravated by the malfunction of a simple basement tool known as a "sump pump." With a name like that, wouldn't you guess it to be annoying? But it seems it's a necessary evil in any basement. So bear with me while I explain how this device actually contributed to messing us up even more. Here's a lesson on the *sump pump*.

To begin with, all basements leak, some, with just a little seepage here and there, others, a lot more. So if the basement leaks, there's an invention to correct the problem: enter, the sump pump!

When basement flooding happens regularly and to solve dampness where the water table is above the foundation of a home, this little miracle sends water away from a house to any place where it is no longer an issue, such as a municipal storm drain. It generally does that by allowing the pump in the floor of the basement to gauge the level of water entering near the foundation and dispensing it through a pipe in the wall. A simple, silly device to cause a divisive issue in a marriage? I'm ashamed to say, it happened.

First, the original pump in the basement when we moved in was not working properly. Hence, there was a sizeable leak at one end of the floor, enough to endanger the safety of ten boxes containing important books. We spoke to the apartment management about it and they agreed to fix the problem.

The people in charge of servicing made the decision to replace the pump with a new one. They installed it and it appeared to work. Only problem was that it solved the leaking but made loud and strange noises 24 hours a day, including nighttime.

Neither Ginny nor I could sleep. That quantity of sleep deprivation didn't help our temperaments, making us more and more cranky. Little things like short, snotty answers to legitimate questions, the silent treatment to avoid conversations, and other behavioral actions that were inconsistent with our large measure of love and respect for one another.

Frankly, I grew tired of making age-related excuses for my own insolence and impatience. It wasn't like me to treat Ginny any way but lovingly. I knew all she had been through to make this move work, and we were both still blaming our age on inexcusable negativity.

So we made a pact, over a late evening of tea by candlelight, of course. Admitting our personal shortcomings was a good start. That led to a few tears, handholding and squeezing and a kiss or two. And we were fixed.

The conclusion to the sump pump dilemma was for me to have a long talk with management and explain how we felt about the effects of a malfunctioning piece of equipment on our temperaments and marital stability. "Please, fix it," I said firmly put politely.

My complaint was accepted with apologies, action was taken, and we received yet another major servicing call that fixed what was broken. Once again, it proved that our practice of working things out verbally and reasonably rather than complaining about them, was still the most effective manner to resolve adverse human conditions and collisions.

There were, of course, other things, too. We had trouble agreeing on any subject. For certain, prior to the move, such times were rare and our friends found our current behavior incredulous. We were even stingy with our show of affection. We were backing ourselves into a dangerous corner.

When we had taken our vows of marriage, we meant every word we said. There was no way that we were ever going change our minds about that. There would never be promiscuous actions or betrayals of any kind. For each of us, what we were doing through public indiscretions was totally above-board, although it sometimes smacked of flirtation with others. We quickly put an end to that!

When we admitted sorrow to one another, we agreed that it served as a mere test that solidified our marriage. We instantly regained the true love we once had, manifest it by returning to cuddling in bed and holding hands wherever we went together. Regardless of our age, and perhaps *because* of it, that was enough for both of us. We had more pressing needs.

The guilt we shared over brief social encounters and indiscretions was a catalyst that drove us back into each other's arms. We savored the feeling of fresh love and appreciated each other more than ever. It was the beginning of a brand new day, a new time of trust in our lives together.

CHAPTER EIGHT

A Second Look

Flashback! It was the day after Christmas, just last year, in 2018. Ginny and I were sitting in the family room recalling some of the highlights and lowlights of the recent Holiday season.

She surprised me with a statement that was uncharacteristically bold for her, especially early in the morning.

"I've been thinking a lot about something lately and I've been hesitant to mention it," she said. My words stepped on hers as I jumped to reply.

"Go ahead," I said, not having a clue about the cataclysmic statement she was about to make.

"Well," she went on, "I've been thinking that I'd like to move back to St. Louis! I miss our kids and I know they've had lonely Christmas's too. And I just think we should move back to be with them."

I didn't need more than a swallow to respond. "You know something," I asked rhetorically, "I couldn't agree with you more!" And that was it! It was that simple. She was shocked that I agreed so quickly and obligingly.

And here it is . . . here we are, four months later and moved into an apartment in St. Louis. After so much time has passed, now I'm beginning to have doubts about the veracity of the decision. Maybe I *should* have objected. How come there was no conscientious objector in all of this, someone to disagree and have an opposing point-of-view?

Oh, well. We can speculate about all sorts of things; but the one fact Ginny and I agree on is that the decision has left us a little disappointed. Not badly, just a little. I guess we thought we'd see more of our kids than we have. We had visions of them dancing through the streets, singing hymns of praise to us for trying to make their lives better. In our minds eye, all of this was in slow motion with millions of tears raising the streams and rivers.

Realistically, however, we knew they had their own lives to live and that by now they'd grown accustomed to seeing our faces around their homes as well as ours. So the newness had worn off.

But besides that, there's a kind of cosmic phenomenon going on within Ginny and me. We think it's related to being so near to our birthplace in Chicago. It's no wonder that we recall things about our childhood more frequently than ever.

We feel closer to so many memories from our past, a lot closer than we ever felt in Florida. Or maybe it's because of the same weather pattern we share, those Midwest fronts that climb across the Rockies, skirt across the plains, and affect both St. Louis and Chicago, like seasonal storms.

In short, there's a feeling that makes us a little more comfortable up here right now. I guess that's it . . . the surroundings are more familiar. And the fact that we raised most of our kids in St. Louis and we used to travel to Chicago often to visit their grandparents and the cultural amenities. Anyway, it's nice to feel closer to what we call "home."

Actually, I hate to admit this, but sometimes, I think we get pretty *excited* about being here. Yeah, excited. In Florida, we used to feel so far away, and we *were*, like 1,500 *miles away.*

But as the kids were growing up in St. Louis, when we drove up to Chicago, we'd visit not only grandparents, but museums, restaurants, malls, with all the "big city" stuff that Florida couldn't compete with . . . theatres, shopping, entertainment, and quite a beautiful great lake on top of all that.

So we seem to be coming around. To say we actually get *excited,* hey, that's pretty good for being 83 and 84, don't you think. But lest we get carried away, we've got to still be practical and realistic. We've got to pay attention to our health.

To date, we haven't checked in with any local Doctors in the St. Louis area. But we should. I've mentioned before that we each have some ailments that slow us down and should be addressed. Nothing critical, but things that can and should be tended to. So we'll do that soon. We both feel like we've got some good years left in us and we know we must do our part to keep ourselves going.

Speaking of which, I've got to pause and tell you about a dream I had last night. It was definitely related to the things I've been talking about, i.e., nearness to our birthplace, good health, aging, etc.

Well, in my dream, I saw several old friends I knew from Chicago. I grew up with their kids so I knew the mom and dad quite well. In fact, my dad was business partners with one of the guys. By now, all of these people have passed away.

Anyway, in my dream, I see my mom and dad and these two old friends. And they're talking very quietly in the corner of a dark restaurant. All of them were dressed nicely so I assume it was a pretty fancy place. But they were all so quiet. And they appeared as if in a hazy mist. It was eerie but I wasn't afraid.

So this guy, this partner of my dad's, starts talking about death and dying. His first question was, "If you had a choice, how'd you like to go? Would you rather go *quickly,* like within a few days of an illness, or would you rather have a few years to settle all your accounts, so to speak, to make the rounds and say farewell to all your old friends and people in your family?" He asks this silly question of all the people at the table.

Well, I didn't like the line of questioning. The guy didn't have a lot of respect for my dad or my mom and I thought his question was pointless since my parents had both been gone for more than ten years and the answer was, well, pointless. So I explained those feelings to the man and also to my mom and dad who were still listening.

Oh, I forgot to mention that I was part of the scene, invisible but a curious participant in the dialogue. I wanted to know how my parents felt about the way they died, both taking several years of illness to pass on. And here was this guy pressing them for answers to questions that had no relevance.

Finally, while all the people in the scene chatted quietly together, I interrupted and got everyone's attention. "Why are you all discussing this meaningless topic," I asked. "First of all, you're all already dead, and secondly, none of you had any choice in how or when you died. So why are you pressing so hard for an answer?"

"We're just curious," the friend said. "We don't have a lot of things to talk about here and we thought we'd see how everyone felt about, well, about God's way of choosing when and how they left their loved ones behind."

I shook my head in disbelief. His answer didn't make any sense to me. But it left me wondering about it. How would I like to go, if I had a choice? And that's when I woke up.

I looked at Ginny sound asleep beside me in bed and appreciated seeing her breathing so well and even sort-of smiling as if she was enjoying her dream. I lay there motionless, opening my eyes and focusing slowly on objects in the room as the sun began to shine on them through a window.

I think I was actually still asleep but I didn't want to wake up. The dream wasn't unhappy, just bewildering. Why couldn't everyone (including me) simply accept God's method of taking us. So I felt like I was clearly getting close to dying and that I had to arrive at a choice for how and when to go. And that frightened me.

I only mention the dream because it clarifies how uncertain Ginny and I had become about . . . well, about everything connected to the past couple of months. We could not make sound decisions, we didn't like being forced to make them, and we were completely lost as far as making them confidently.

None of that made me feel any better. And I had to explain every part of the dream to Ginny when she awakened. Perhaps she'd have a different spin on it all. Or, maybe, she'd be even more confused than I was. We agreed that the dream indicated to both of us how stressed we were in being forced to make so many tough calls, serious decisions. It's just as if we *doubted* every once in awhile if maybe we were too old to face such things. But then again, maybe not.

So all we learned from this *pause* was that we were still uncertain about whether to remain in St. Louis and make the thing work for us, or whether to consider picking up stakes and heading back to what we thought was *Paradise*. How could we possibly still be so uncertain after all we'd been through? It was mind-boggling!

CHAPTER NINE

The Third Partner

Ginny and I have died and gone to heaven!

We are convinced that this is the right place.

Sure, there were a few detours and lapses in reasoning, but we *are* in the right place. We are certain. But how did this come about? I have only one answer: I finally allowed myself to heal!

Being fair about it, we give credit where credit is due. We trusted in Almighty God and He did not let us down. He was the important "third partner" Who guided us to the climactic pot of gold at the end of the rainbow. He was a caring friend.

Oh, it took a while to part the clouds of confusion so we could see the path more clearly, but we recognize that it was our faith in God, our *trust* in His Son that brought us to a final conclusion. It was completely our fault to doubt Him, but now that we've come to our senses, we've concluded that this is it, emphatically . . . St. Louis forever.

There was a particular day and time when the turnabout occurred. Mark yesterday. It was yesterday at a morning Mass at St. Clare of

Assisi Parish on the western edge of Ballwin, a suburb of St. Louis. Here's how our malaise came to an end.

Maybe I can explain it with a graphic metaphor. It was spring in St. Louis when we moved here. And spring is a very wet season with tons of rain, miles of flooding, and a day that typically starts out in the upper 40's. But as the day progresses, the clouds separate, the skies brighten, and the temperature reaches between 60 or 70 degrees. So when I get up and head for Church every morning, it's chilly, damp and dark. I have to wear an extra layer of clothing to be comfortable.

But then, characteristically, all that changes. It slowly warms into the mid-70's and sometimes into the 80's, all in the same day. Generally, it turns into a beautiful day with blooming green trees and lush flowers against a blue sky. It becomes a perfect day, but only after residents pay their dues.

Similarly, as we matured from a chrysalis and drew fresh air, we metaphorically became more comfortable, prepared to experience a *perfect* St. Louis day. It's uncanny, really, and you have to witness it to believe it. That's where God came in.

Ginny and I were born and baptized as Roman Catholics. Through our 83 and 84 years, we've been absolutely faithful to the laws and tenets of that faith, not *perfect*, you understand, but obedient to the laws of Jesus Christ and His Church. And the gift of faith is the driver of how we obey the rules. Oh, it's not easy and it doesn't come without some days that are dark and chilly and nasty.

But as the days of early spring morphed into clarity, our faith did the same. We finally saw the light of a bright sun and colorful blossoms against a blue sky. We were overcome, overwhelmed to spring forth into emotional action, passionately shouting out, "It's the end of another seasonal storm. We see the light! St. Louis is the place for us. No doubts ever again."

Honestly, that's how we compare our resignation to God's will, our acceptance of all that St. Louis offers, and the lowest of the lows up to the highest of the highs. We accept all of them. Perhaps, we wonder, does nature actually mimic the moods of the human populace? Now we've learned that we can handle it all. Since that wonderful experience yesterday morning, I'm ready to accept anything the Lord hands me.

About that Mass. When I first entered Church around 8:00am, I noticed that there were school children occupying the front rows of pews. And they were dressed so uniformly with red, pleated skirts and white blouses for the girls and dark blue shorts with white shirts for the boys. Uniformly!

Most important, the eight grades of students behaved as they were dressed, consistently perfect, obeying the spiritual, traditional rules of the Holy Mass just as it was done centuries ago.

And I was touched by that . . . silent, well-clothed young people reverently following the lead of the Pastor of the Parish. And such a *leader* he is.

In unison with his actions, I personally emerged from the chrysalis of sub-conscious adolescence. Everything that had bothered me before suddenly became a benefit, a plus, a major point in favor of St. Louis as the place for us to live-out the remainder of our days.

It amazed me to analyze how much a role *perspective* played in my life. Perspective! It had changed everything. So many elements of life in the Midwest that had irked me, suddenly became acceptable, even beautiful. The winding, sinewy roads I had complained about had become so much more interesting than the straight roads of Florida.

The squirrels bounding across our backyard trees knocking down leaves and disturbing all the songbirds has changed from *pesty critters* into *part of the natural scene.* And the consistent puddles filling the sidewalks were transformed into homes for tiny insects that helped to nourish the grass. All of it had become an enjoyable fascination rather than an immovable objection.

And much of that had to do with *attitude.* Remember how much emphasis I had placed on *attitude* near the front of my story when I was belly-aching about everything that wasn't quite right?

At that time, I blamed *attitude* for increased anxiety and reduced acceptance, a lot of negatives and shrinking consent. Attitude was given a broad brushstroke of blame. But then, by implementing a stronger, more accurate *perspective* of the Midwest and all its amenities, everything fell into place. The bottom line was happiness and contentment.

To say the least, once I got my head together, it affected Ginny's outlook as well as my own. In essence, she became a much happier person. And that was my goal from the very start. I never bought into the old bromide, "Happy wife, happy life." But I learned that there was, indeed, *something* to it.

At the risk of making this sound like a tourism plug since I've learned the art of fair play, I note and appreciate the recreational enhancements of the area. To name only a handful: the Art Museum of St. Louis, the famous Zoo, the Science Museum, and a list of wonderful small towns surrounding the city in what's known as "The Wine Country." That area stretches through the western countryside, even east into southern Illinois. It's abundant with vineyards and wineries and restaurants that offer a soothing ambience as well as delicious meals indigenous to the historic area.

A few other comments about our Church, a pivotal factor in my personal acceptance of our new home. Over 300 children attend the Parish School. And boy, do they know how to sing. During that important morning Mass I attended, they had a choir of children that sang so beautifully they brought me to tears. And there was a small boy who contributed by playing a large set of drums. Of course, the incongruity with a piano made me smile and helped me appreciate the contribution of musical children. Their heavenly sound calmed me.

During this upbeat time in our lives, I am continually fascinated by natural elements like rain, clouds, flooding, lightning, thunder, all exerting human influence on my behavior. Each and every one of those sometimes alters my mood. Some work in my behalf while others fight against me.

Ever think about that? Notice some time and observe how your mood can be changed by elements of nature. In English literature, there is a practice known as "pathetic fallacy." It is a literary device in which human emotions are attributed to nature. For example, one can say "the *angry* storm" and it can serve as the foreground of a violent act. That's basically what I'm noticing. And most of it is for the better, for better human moods that turn frowns into smiles. On a lot of people, not just me.

I'm noticing an awful lot of that these happier days. I only wish I could have made this discovery a long time ago. It's so effective in making my life happier and, as a result, Ginny's, too. I really feel like I'm improving as a person . . . and it all started by moving to St. Louis in a sort-of opposite momentum shift after our 62 years of married life.

Just yesterday, Ginny reminded me in her subtle and beautiful way: "Do you realize what we've done here in two months? We have entirely changed our lives, everything, from the climate to our diets. We've changed it all. And so far, we're surviving. Did you think this was really possible?"

I had to spend some 30 seconds allowing the question to resonate. "Yeah," I said. "I do think I'm aware of what we've done, against what a lot of people predicted, even close friends who said we were crazy and that it'd never work."

"I know we were never out to *prove* them wrong, either. I mean, that was not our focus," Ginny replied, then continued, "I was too busy coping, trying to make everything fit into a neat little package. Until you helped turn things around the other day with your "visions" at Church. Boy, was that ever an "assist" that came from nowhere."

"Now, sweetheart," I said quickly. "You know that came from some *One*, not some *where*. And I'm glad you recognize that it was a huge turning point. It transformed all my doubt back into trust, a complete *trust* in God, a surrender, so to speak, back to the kind of faith I had all my life."

"Amen!" That was all she said.

But I picked it up again by saying, "Trust and doubt, they're so closely related and yet they're the opposite of one another. Hard to figure."

"But we sure covered *both* of them while we were sorting this out, didn't we?" I said. Ginny agreed, leading us to a related subject that we had not intended to examine so thoroughly.

The conversation caused me to examine the *meaning* of trust. Webster says, "Trust is a transcendent fundamental or spiritual reality." It had to be simpler than that. How about, "A firm belief in the reliability, truth, strength, and obligation of someone." (I think that last one covers God.)

For most of my life, trust *did* relate to God more than anything else. Of course, it was attached to parents, siblings, and so forth. But when I trusted in *God,* I sincerely believed He would answer my prayer. God would address my request, make a judgment, and reach a fair conclusion.

What most of us want when we pray is an answer that's positive. God says, "Yes!" And the prayer is granted, in a suitable time-frame. Yes, prayers are usually *favors* we're asking of God. So it's not uncommon for someone who asks God for a favor to then receive a positive answer.

Which brings us down to applying trust to having ones prayers answered by God. We trusted that God would hear our prayer and grant us joy and happiness in St. Louis. We did it for the right reason, to be closer to our children in case of need, both ours and theirs. Our motives weren't selfish, not much, anyway. We wanted to be happy because *they* were happy.

CHAPTER TEN

More Trust

Clearly, it was our faith and *trust* in God that got us this far, to the cusp of fulfillment and joy. It took a lot of hard work to get here, but He answered our prayer. Now the question was, would it last? Would and could I remain consistent enough to support God's will for the rest of my life, thus making St. Louis our permanent home . . . without changing my mind all over again. I'd do my best!

While we're still on the subject, allow me to apply *trust* to one additional topic, the sale of our house in Fort Myers. From the start, we had faith and trust in God to answer our prayer for a fast and painless detachment of that house, at a fair price and within at least six months. That didn't seem unreasonable at the time, but as we consume more and more of that, that's where the issue of doubt comes into play. I doubted that God was going to answer my prayer immediately . . . and I was right!

For some reason, yet to be determined and not revealed to us, the house just won't sell. Like I explained at the beginning, we signed with an excellent realtor but it appears as though other factors have played a part in our disappointment, factors like the Fort Myers economy.

So God's put our request on hold for the time being. And it's depressing for both Ginny and me. There's a decent piece of money tied up down there and we need it up here, like right now. Now, God is testing our patience (as He's known to do from time to time). But this time, He's really pushing hard. So I'm again on the precipice of exhaustion and ready to jump into a chasm of despair.

No, I won't forget my recent commitment to *trust.* I'll stick by my Leader and trust that He has a good reason to delay things. For sure, at the end, He'll reveal His wisdom, and once again, Ginny and I will be believers with gratitude and understanding.

But what if He sees something in the future that would harm us if we sold the house now. He can do that, you know, see things in the future and protect those He loves from making big mistakes. Don't we want Him to stop us now if He sees the time just isn't right?

There I go again, connecting doubt with trust. You can see how the two are linked and how confusing it gets. Can I trust the Lord to give me what I want . . . no, I can't, because He does things His own way . . . and He might decide we should wait to sell the house until later in the year or something like that. Bottom line? He knows what's best for us and He'll protect us from ourselves.

My, oh, my. How complex these things get. I'm actually questioning if we *are* too old to continue working on this until it reaches a climactic end. So if we trust in God and allow everything to run its course, it'll all work out. And we'll continue to be happy in St. Louis. I know that for sure. It's part of my trust contract with God. I've got to do my part if I expect Him to do His.

Right now, it's nearing sundown and I'm distracted by the song of a small bird right at my open window. Sounds maybe like a tree sparrow or something tiny like that. It's fluttering around a limb that touches my window. The bird likes it there and comes around a lot. He's a happy little fellow and wants for nothing but God's gift to him each and every day.

I'm reminded of the quote from Jesus, "Look at the birds of the air," He once said, " . . . for they neither sow nor reap nor gather into barns; yet your heavenly Father feeds them. Are you not of more value than they?" What a response. God is saying that to me right now. If I have trust in His care like the little bird does, He will care for Ginny and me and every one of our children. Now *that's* a sizeable reward for trusting. No doubt, with a little faith, too.

By the way, this day marks the second month that we've been here. And when I think back, we've come a long way. The boxes . . . oh, how we hated those boxes, 180 of them stacked to the ceiling in almost every room of the house . . . and to the far corners of the basement.

They were too heavy to lift so we had to push and slide them from place to place. It never failed that a box marked "bedroom" had to be moved to its farthest place in the kitchen, and vice versa. Then, the unloading of that cumbersome box was arguably as demanding as getting the box to the correct room.

I think it was partially due to the way items were packed. We'd unwrap a mountain of paper from something as small as a set of earrings . . . or four sheets of *butcher paper* from a single book. The effort was exhausting and time-consuming. But now, we're nearly finished and we can actually see from wall-to-wall in every room.

Incidentally, we did hire the *College Hunks* who systematically carried off some of the clutter in the basement. They were very efficient and the cost was reasonable. It helped us to feel some progress.

Back to the Fort Myers house that won't sell. We just can't understand it. It's 19 years old and in near-perfect condition. We maintained it very conscientiously and received compliments on how nice it looked. Praise generally came from people who were interested in buying to passers-by who drove through as they canvassed the neighborhood.

Now, the realtor receives complaints from visitors like, "We want a house with a pool," which our house doesn't have. Another favorite for rejection: "The yellow wall in the living and dining room is too bright!" Never heard that one before.

It's obvious that most reasons for not buying are more like an *excuse* than a *reason.* We're mystified by what to do besides show-case the house every weekend. We can't possibly make every correction to please differing likes and dislikes. We'd go broke!

So "the house that nobody wants" remains an albatross, like a psychological burden that feels like a curse, an allusion to Samuel Taylor Coleridge's poem *The Rime of the Ancient Mariner.* And *that* makes it worthwhile to send a prayer for help. But where is the Lord when we need Him most? Like I said earlier, trust does require patience.

But another factor that's put a dent in our house sale is the Fort Myers housing market in general. Most agree that it's largely due to the 2018 environmental disaster blamed on issues like Red Tide and filthy beaches from runoff of the Lake Okeechobee dam. For close to one year, the dirty beaches and polluted waters have frightened tourists and prospective residents away from visiting and/or buying in the area. The impact has been serious.

Ginny and I have come to the conclusion that our house not selling is yet another experience from which we're learning. And since we can only build on the experience before us in life, we've observed so much in just a couple of months that we would never have known if we didn't do this. That alone is satisfying. It makes it worthwhile. Imagine learning new things, tons of them based on new experiences, at our age.

There are so many times in a day when I say to myself, "I never would've seen that gorgeous little girl with her class in Church this morning. She was just precious, the way she smiled at her teacher." And to realize in that one little moment that I wouldn't have seen that if we had stayed in Florida.

Couple of days ago, there was a, probably an eight-year-old boy, teasing a girl of the same age as they danced and laughed their way through the supermart, mother chasing them up and down the aisles. They were having such an enjoyable time. I just treasured that. It was wonderful to observe and I knew I had God to thank for it, some little piece of life that I never would have seen before.

You know something, compared to up here, we just didn't see that many children in Florida. Because they're not there. They're up here, across the Midwest, in the schools and stores and shops and everywhere you look. We missed kids down there. The major portion of the people are older folks like Ginny and me. And we missed the experience of watching kids have fun as they grow and learn. I'm getting really proud that we had the guts, the courage, whatever you want to call it, we had that, we took a big risk, and so far, we're so much happier for it.

I guess most people our age wouldn't be interested in risking all they had to go off on a whim and just hope for the best. Though I don't feel our decision was irresponsible, we did recognize that it was risky. We both knew it could prove disastrous. We could've lost a lot of our money just paying for the movers, for example.

And I think, too, that the risks ran deeper than money. We assessed the level of happiness we had achieved in Fort Myers and it was measureable, sizeable. But what if we couldn't find that level of joy "up north." What if that happened? We'd have no one to blame but ourselves.

Thoughts like those do crop up once in awhile. And for the most part, they please us because we know that we were responsible for our own success, with God's help, of course.

So many wise people buy into the notion that "We are responsible for our own good time." Ginny and I believe that. Over all the years of raising seven kids into adulthood we practiced that, passed it on to our kids, "We are responsible for our own good time." If we're not happy, the blame for that failure falls right back on our own shoulders. If we're unhappy, then it's most likely our own fault. Some of that surely lies in the fact that as a species, we're generally unwilling to take risks.

It's an awesome thought to go back over these past two months and try to list all the learning we've done. I'll tell you what, the real way I can tell is by reviewing all the sleepless nights. There's so much tumult going on in my head when I lay it on the pillow. I really do have trouble sleeping. But they're not nightmares. It's just that I struggle with so many things that need a lot of serious attention. Yes, there's still a ton of decision-making going on inside of me.

It's no wonder that Ginny and I have not gained a single pound since the move. In fact, we've kept our weight under perfect control by maintaining the same as when we flew out of Florida. That in itself is a commendable and healthful achievement.

Moreover, I have a daily goal . . . to introduce Ginny to something new, usually for lunch. I mostly choose to make it a restaurant in the city of St. Louis, a place with a reputation for . . . anything: the biggest, the finest, the quickest, the cheapest, the hottest, the coldest, the oldest, etc. We both enjoy that so much and it's another avenue of learning from a new experience. And every one of those experiences is done *together!*

Speaking of *together.* Never has there been any time in our lives when we've spent more minutes, hours and days together in the same room. I mean that's saying a lot for us, people who've seen a lot of one another over 63 years. For the most part, it's okay. But it gets a little hairy when we clash over tiny things. Here's an example of what I'm talking about.

It seems that the little things do count. If I dare to move a vase, for example, one inch in any direction from its original place, Ginny moves it back, mostly a distance so slight that only a trained eye like mine could detect it.

It's uncanny how it works both ways. When she moves something, just barely budges it, I'll notice and say something about it, or *not* say anything about it and just inch it back to its first position. Why do we do that? We've talked about it as a new phenomenon between us. We have no answer for it. But it continues.

If I could accurately document the instances at which that has occurred, it would fill a dozen pages of this book. In fact, it would be so consistent that it would be boring and maddening at the same time. I believe it's the predictability that drives us crazy. And we don't do it to be cruel or mean . . . we just do it. I could bet money on it every time. If I pass a magazine on the coffee table and adjust it ever so slightly to correct its vertical/horizontal alignment, I know it'll be changed by the time I return.

In most cases, we laugh it off. But there *have* been a few instances when one of us reaches the boiling point . . . and simply explodes! No swearing, just glaring, to silently display anger. The only conclusion we've reached is that it's an obsession rather than a habit . . . an obsession!

CHAPTER ELEVEN

Memories

Since we've been amassing so many new memories for our personal archives, Ginny and I have also spent some time reminiscing about our past. We started out as most young couples do, with a passion to travel the world, but not the foggiest notion of how, when, or why. But alas! To make a long story short, I was involved in the motion picture industry at a very early age, then majored in English in College and ended up owning my own media business from the ages of 35 to 65. And that business, because of its very nature, allowed us to see the world . . . on someone else's budget.

It was a great perk that we deeply appreciated for 30 years. Fortunately, our oldest son, Daniel, joined me in the business and provided the necessary support for those talents I was short on, i.e., the technical side of photography, computer programming, movie-making, staging, live entertainment. He was a gifted friend who brought both fun and financial success to the small business.

The bottom line of all that was the fact that our expertise combined to produce sales meetings for many of America's largest companies, namely, AT&T, General American Life Insurance,

Monsanto, Northwestern National Life, Emerson Electric Company and many others.

In those days, the reward for a persons sales excellence was to win a trip to an exotic destination somewhere beyond the limits of North America. And while we delivered the *sizzle* for those elaborate meetings, Dan and Ginny and I necessarily had to travel on-site to entertain the winners. And that was where the perk of travel entered the picture.

In the 30 years that the business provided us with a living, we experienced a marvelous and exciting itinerary of the world. We traveled to all the capitols of every European nation, most of the Caribbean islands, destinations in the far East including Hong Kong, China, Thailand, the island of Bali in Indonesia, and multiple trips to each of the beautiful islands of Hawaii.

So it's not like we hadn't seen the world before we arrived in St. Louis. Not at all. The only reason I mention our travel is the fact that it provided us with an appreciation of what ethnic diversity was all about while it provided us with a mental overview that allowed us to appreciate the International flavor of a fascinating part of American culture named after a great French General, Saint Louis.

As proof that things are still a bit awkward and disorganized around here, I offer this as a shining example. If you're up to it, bear with me and try to follow an accurate conversation between me and a Physician's office I'm trying to contact. These are the exact words of my phone call that was answered by the Doctor's associate assigned to booking new patients. I was referred by a friend who is a current patient of the Physician.

Me: "Hi, I've just relocated here and I'd like to make an appointment to see the Doctor as soon as possible."

Her: "Will you be a first-time patient here?"

Me: "Yes, I just told you. I've relocated here and this will be my first visit."

Her: "Have you ever been here before?"

Me: "Could you please tell me when the first available date is?"

Her: "What kind of insurance do you have?"

Me: "It's Medicare and as a supplement, it's United Healthcare of Missouri."

Her: "What's your date-of-birth and full name as it appears on Medicare?"

Me: (Provide name, address, phone, SS#, etc.)

Her: "The first opening I have is August 10th."

Me: "But that's three months away."

Her: "I have nothing sooner."

Me: "Okay, I'll take it. I have one other request. My previous Doctor in Florida said if I wanted my records forwarded, I could give you their FAX number and they'd be happy to do that. I'd like the Doctor to read my past history and treatments before I see him. Could you take care of that for me?"

Her: "I'm sorry, we cannot initiate that request. You have to call them and have them FAX the information. But first, you must sign a release when you come in to see us."

Me: "I signed a release at my previous Doctor's office before I left and they said that's all they need to FAX my stuff."

Her: "Not enough. You must *initiate* the request before we can ask for the information. Here's our FAX number."

Me: "They explained to me clearly that it's *you* who must make the request and then they'll respond."

Her: "That's not the way we operate, sir."

Me: "So I'm requesting my records to be sent to your office, isn't that correct?"

Her: "Of course, if that's what you want."

This inane exchange went on for 25 minutes. I was an inch from screaming out loud but knew it was just part of the price of *transferring records* to other Doctors, especially across State lines.

The Q and A actually got so bad that I cancelled everything and politely explained that I'd be going somewhere else for my treatment. I figured that if the Physician's *office* was that bad, I'd rather not take any chances with the man running the show.

Eventually, I found a good professional Physician for both myself and Ginny and we now feel secure in having medical care with an adjacent hospital to support our residency. I guess it all "went with the territory" of relocation and simply became another segment of our *moving* trials.

My gosh, there's my visiting bird friend again, sitting on his favorite branch outside my window. I think he can actually *see* me and enjoys hearing the sound of the clicking keys of the computer.

He's turning his head back and forth now. My additional research tells me he's most probably what they call a *Swanson's Warbler* but ornithologists claim that bird is extremely shy and prefers remote habitats. This one's an odd bird, all right, but I enjoy his visits, even though he *does* interrupt my concentration.

On this day, I literally lost it, my mind, that is. I was driving alone down a beautiful winding street when I lost my mind, quickly found it, and hopelessly reminisced. In short, I had a *"slip."*

Now when an alcoholic makes a commitment to stop drinking and he sticks to it for a long time, he/she is given a lot of credit. Because that kind of discipline requires an abundance of strength. But if that same person goes on a binge, over-drinks for one night of partying, it's called a *"slip."* Either he let his guard down, forgot to focus, or just lost sight of his goal.

Well, today, I had a *"slip"* regarding my devotion to St. Louis. No, I didn't over-drink a lot of alcohol, but I had a lot on my mind, things weren't going very well and I was fighting a pretty bad infection. So I lost my focus and let myself *"slip"* into some feelings of self-pity. For a few minutes, I recalled some of my fondest memories of favorite places in Florida. Actually, I got a bit chocked up. And I remembered that it was once said that, "Nostalgia is a fond memory."

One of my favorite places to be privately nostalgic was in the nearby town of Naples, about an hours drive south of Fort Myers. I'd drop Ginny off in the city and spend some time just ambling around quiet, hidden, secret spots where I enjoyed getting lost. Some would call it an "escape."

Well, this one was near the south end of the city of Naples, a very wealthy town full of very rich people who were a bit on the snobbish side. And they deserved to be. For they had it all, more money than they knew how to spend, homes that averaged between 5 and 10 million dollars, boats that could cost the same, and a lazy lifestyle they had earned over many years of hard work and wise investing.

So when I had my "alone time" in that place, I'd find some of the hiding places of those rich and famous people, cautious not to make my presence too obvious for fear they'd label me as a phony and ride me out of town. In the first place, I didn't dress like them. I preferred faded old T-shirts while others lounged in designer shirts and shorts. I refused to honor the ostentatiously wealthy elitists.

One of my hiding spots was a restaurant and bar called, *"The Dock."* All seating was outside, of course, because there really was no rain to worry about. There always seemed to be clear skies and warm water teeming with fish of all kinds and sizes, not for catching but just for watching and admiring.

Well, there was also a long, peaceful dock in that secret place. It was my pleasure to slowly walk the dock, pausing to chat with a fisherman or two, sniffing the aroma of fresh saltwater from the Gulf, and enjoying a cold, refreshing beer while sitting with my feet dangling over the edge of the pier.

That's what I was picturing when I let myself *"slip."* All of my senses enjoyed the pleasures and I felt no guilt whatsoever. I hadn't savored a moment like that since we moved to St. Louis. And I knew I'd suffer for it. I had come so far in forgetting such natural beauty and appreciating new places in St. Louis. I knew it would take a while to get back on track, just like that alcoholic who "slipped" and had a hard time getting his head back together.

In short, this was my day for enjoying a weakness and becoming self-absorbed in memories of almost 20 years in paradise. There was nothing wrong with that. I mean, it wasn't exactly a moral failure. More like a lapse. Had I betrayed Ginny? Would she be hurt by that? I would apologize to make sure she wasn't. She quickly accepted.

That was about the time when I recalled some best friends that I had made in Fort Myers. They were about my age or older and it was an important time in my life as it was in theirs.

It began with an invitation to join a circle of retired gentlemen who respectfully called themselves *The Coffeeboys.* From my first session on, I had quite a ride, mostly observing, occasionally contributing, always appreciating conversations that were anything but mundane.

The listening was easy. And because the conversation was so flavorful and healthful, digestion was assured. There were adventurous tales of the past, profound appraisals of the present, and bold prognostications of the future, all enriched by a tasty seasoning of humor.

A good memory was also an essential component. There's a saying, "Those who cannot remember the past are condemned to repeat it." Well, to be sure, these men remembered the past quite well, were not willing to repeat it, and relished every moment that remained. And that left a lot of conversation to be spoken and assimilated.

Unusually, the toxic divisions which rive a polarized nation were unwelcome at this table. Here, there was more harmony than discord, more conciliation than argument. No boasting and no showing off. In a culture of victimhood, these men were secure enough to blame no one or anything for unfortunate events in their lives.

Hence, within the mix of once-successful businessmen and entrepreneurs, handshakes were in, hugs out, tears in, frowns out, jokes in, gossip out. They believed in the Irish saying, "He who gossips *with* you, gossips *of* you." And at this point in life, no one was willing to take the risk.

One of the happiest and hardiest of the lot, a man who spends at least half his life making people laugh, lost his older brother in the Korean War, both parents early in his life, his 31-year-old son in an auto accident, his wife to cancer, his sister to heart disease, and he served as a caregiver for his younger brother who predeceased him. I've yet to hear him complain or partake in self-pity. He accepts God's will, is at peace with himself, and enjoys just about anyone's company.

Without exception, each of *The Coffeeboys* is so unselfish that he'd be the last one off a sinking ship. The only way one finds out about a person's illness in this group is to hear it from a spouse or another friend. No one speaks of personal health problems. Never! No whiners allowed.

Something else. Within these sessions, each man finds it as easy to cry as to laugh. And the tears are commonly tears of joy rather than sorrow. But the diversity of things cried over is amazing, including but not limited to: happy endings, weddings, injustice, the loss of family or friends, tragedies in the news, stories of goodness in the world, poverty, hunger, war, cures for anything, and reminiscing about happy times.

Unarguably, the essential fuel that keeps *The Coffeeboys* running is compassion; a close second is love; third is the desire for peace in the world. Surely, in the microcosm of their small Florida community, sturdy minds and big hearts are actively peacing the world together.

As for me? Well, I was always just a fan in the grandstand, cheering the team on as it took its daily swings and watching teammates hit the long ball. I was, indeed, privileged to be a spectator at the daily sessions of *The Coffeeboys.*

At this writing, only three of the original group are alive and only one remains in Fort Myers, the last of a breed of men who were proud to be only themselves. I miss all of them deeply. It was the most memorable time of my life for friendships.

Would that I could replace each of them with similar souls in St. Louis. But it's not meant to be. So I resign myself to a blissful memory accepted with gratitude as simply, "Once in a Lifetime."

CHAPTER TWELVE

A Retrospective

As I was growing in age through all of this, I realized that Ginny and I were approaching the last years of our life. No denying it. Me at 84 and her at 83 . . . no matter how you sliced it, the time for passing on was closer now than ever before.

When I look at relatives these days, even our own children for that matter, I face the reality that in another 25 to 30 years, not a single person I know or care about will be here. Every one of us will have ceased to be. And who'll be here to take their place? Gosh, I don't have a clue. Does anyone else?

Ginny and I now face that reality as the aches and pains progress to more than minor annoyances. Some have affected our lifestyle and the ability to get around to do our shopping and eating in restaurants. Some have limited our mobility through the many strains of arthritis, cartilage breakdown, muscle inflammation, sciatica, stenosis. But those are still the easy ones because they aren't terminal, just painful and discomforting.

But every disease introduced to us requires a Physician and a response to help us stay alive. Nobody ever explained how difficult this would be. We had such a wonderful life together over many years and it saddens us to see it coming to a end.

Always the question of wondering . . . who is likely to go first? It's most unlikely that we'll die together. So how will the survivor make it without his/her spouse. Certainly, difficult times are upon us as we plod through our 80's and perhaps even 90's.

But at least we're still together and deeply in love; and neither requires any special care like that of a nursing home. So far, we've been spared the fears of dreaded shifts in our health.

One night, we stayed up very late and sat at the kitchen table discussing such heavy material. We sat before a slow-burning candle, just like we did when we planned our lives as an engaged couple.

We'd relax there and stare at a small burning flame while sipping hot tea, until we nearly fell asleep holding hands. It was a useful pastime that greatly bred closeness and thus encouraged us to pursue any dream no matter how impossible or impractical it might be.

These days, during similar times of uncertainty, we discuss what's left of our dreams and our ultimate experience after we pass into God's hands. We speculate and most often agree on generic visions of the afterlife while maintaining distinct images of our own.

God has chosen to privately take care of all that. We learned over our years together that no two visions could ever be exactly alike because we humans each have such unique imaginations. There are no matches for identical pictures of the place distinctively called *heaven.* Besides, individual visions spiritualize so differently from anything our earthly minds can possibly create or comprehend. That's the way it was meant to be.

I guess if I was challenged to describe what I think heaven is like, I'd be embarrassed to answer. Have I been so privileged to know something no one else does? I think not. So I can only use conjecture when I point out the following: it must be a beautiful place. But if I picture beauty in our earthly terms, it doesn't make sense if I say waterfalls and rainbows and mountains and flowers . . . those are all composed of earthen materials. And this is *heaven* we're talking about . . . *heaven!*

It's going to be like nothing we've ever seen, glorious and lovely and perfect beyond anything we can imagine. So if we can't *imagine* it, what human tools can we use to bring it to life? None!

There was a wonderful movie that ran in theatres several years ago called "The Shack." In it were conceptual scenes of heaven, many of them typical of traditional conceptions, i.e., fields of flowers, rainbows, forests, etc. It was pretty much the way most people envision it.

But who knows? None of us ever returned to describe it. And the imaginary *heaven* in films may be so far from what actually awaits, that most of those who arrive there will be blown away, simply forced into laughter at the visualizations that are totally inconceivable and unimaginable to us now.

One thing for certain, whatever it *looks* like (assuming human eyes are required to see it), we'll be surprised by what it's like. That's God's game. He wants to surprise us. He wants to play the role of Creator, the One Who made everything from nothing. He wants His reward for the good people to be appropriate, astounding, like nothing we've ever conceived. So why not just give up, surrender to His plan and . . . *be surprised!*

We have no choice, really. Since we have no clue of what He has in His gift bag, we might as well play His game, leave Him alone, and wait for the surprise to occur. Actually, when you think about it, all of that is good reason to behave ourselves and gleefully await death and a second life in an unknown place . . . *heaven!*

We've only got to believe in Him, obey a few simple rules, and we'll have the surprise of a lifetime. Once again, it involves those earthly gifts of patience, faith, and trust.

Back to what's left. It's been a long time since I gave you an update on our St. Louis living accommodations. Maybe I never explained that our apartment is in a complex of buildings that vary in size between two and eight units per block. The sizes range from one bedroom to three bedrooms, some with a basement, like ours.

You might recall that I referred to that basement as "The Graveyard" because it's the place where all of our leftover stuff goes to die. That basement is big all right, as large in square footage as the upstairs living area. So it's got plenty of room to house those big moving boxes we didn't know what else to do with. But it's also big enough to cause a few problems. First, it leaks! (Remember my infamous story of the sump pump?)

Well, spring brought so much rain to the area that the water had no place to go but through holes and cracks. At least it flowed nicely rather than splitting the floor like some basements do. Management is coping with the problem and there's a long waiting list for repairs, with our name near the bottom. We really don't care much since we have our old things spread far enough away from the leaky spots so they aren't hurting anything.

Actually, those are the problems we don't mind passing on to the owners, because it's a selfish, worry-free perk to not be concerned. As with yard work, we had our share of the worries over 60 years of home ownership. It's much easier now to just pick up the phone and have anything fixed with no hassles and no expenses.

So our unit is in a block with only one other apartment which makes neighboring a whole lot better . . . nobody upstairs or down, merely beside us and completely noise proof. The entire complex is about 40 years old and a bit on the worn side, though it's been kept attractive and appealing with frequent repairs. It's primarily made of used red brick and a matching frame facade.

Landscaping is well maintained with plentiful amounts of large trees, flowers, bushes and attractive driveways and walkways. Most of the trees are old and large with some reaching as high as 100 to 200 feet. They include sycamore, oak, ash, fir, and a ton of odorous honeysuckle. It all contributes to lovely areas for walking and resting beside several ponds and a large clubhouse with two swimming pools.

It's really nothing much to boast about, but it's also nothing to be ashamed of. As a matter of fact, we're quite proud to live here with friendly people who share the pride of a well-maintained facility.

We've also spent some time and money fixing up the *inside* with contemporary furniture and modest accoutrements. It's conservative but comfortable and easy to keep clean, especially since lovely Lily continues to be a part of the *breathing* interior landscape. We expect her to be with us for quite awhile. She causes no trouble and is a friendly part of the ambience, blending in nicely, making very little noise, and very affectionate, especially when it comes to her surrogate mother, Ginny.

CHAPTER THIRTEEN

Conflicts

Okay, it's May 10ᵗʰ and it should be nice and warm, right? Wrong! This is St. Louis, remember. Unpredictable spring, 40 on one day, 80 the next. And so on. Rain, rain, rain, with dark, colorless skies. Temperature currently at 42 degrees. And we're supposed to be happy? It's as depressing as any weather on earth. And I think I'm ready for another *"slip,"* one of those lapses when I subconsciously drop off the planet and mentally place myself somewhere I'm not.

Sorry. I can't help this. But I'm reminiscing again, recalling some wonderful time back in *paradise.* I've just dropped Ginny off to do some shopping and I'm alone to visit a favorite spot. This one's a tiny restaurant that graces the rooftop of an upscale store in North Naples. The scene defies description, but I'll give it a shot.

Every customer walks a flight of stairs to get up here. A small bar faces the most beautiful scene you could imagine. It's a bay of blue water, always calm and quiet and lined with expensive homes. Your vision can easily count the lines of an azure swimming pool that dots the lawn behind each home. I'd guess the bay itself is several miles long and one mile wide.

I order a beer and lean my elbows onto the bar. I'm not totally alone. But the great thing about this place is the diversity. There's an unshaven guy on one side of me who looks like he's homeless, and on the other side is a guy who looks like he owns the place, well dressed with sunglasses propped on the top of his head. Both of my neighbors enjoy a beer. But nobody speaks. This is what I like about it here. No conversation. What could a person possibly talk about with all that bounteous luxury spread before him?

The homes bordering the magnificent bay are all multi-million in price. Each has a dock for boats the resident owns. Plural b o a t s. Many of the little things are scurrying about the bay; some are skillfully dodging the dozen-or-so resident dolphin that pop up at indiscriminate places in the water.

And oh, there's music here. A single guitarist strums Jimmy Buffet songs and sings along. I conclude that the guy at the bar who looks like he's homeless is actually the guy who owns the place . . . and the other guy who's dressed like a millionaire is hiding from somebody. I love this place and never want to leave. But Ginny's ready to be picked up so I'd better break my trance.

I'm back in St. Louis, driving on a jam-packed highway during rush hour and cursing every driver who passes me. I'm back to reality. Just in time to see the clouds part and the sky open to sunlight. Yes, this is St. Louis all right and I'm happy to be here (I think). It's a lovely spring day and exactly forty-two degrees. Once again, my *"slip"* didn't hurt anybody. And there was nothing even slightly immoral about it.

Sometimes, I think we miss the point of all this. We came down here in the first place to be around in case our kids needed us. Or, as we first explained to friends, we moved to St. Louis so we'd be happier . . . to be around our children would result in more joy for ourselves. But now, if I'm asked, I wonder exactly who it was for. Was it really for them or was it something selfish we did for ourselves. Tough to answer.

Here's the core of the problem. If we went through all of this hard work with its associated risks for ourselves, then I can understand why we're slightly disgruntled. Because we don't see the kids that much more to give us *increased* joy. And I don't believe we're proportionately happier enough to have made it worthwhile. Does that make sense?

I mean, we did enjoy ourselves in Florida. Sure, there were things that aggravated us. But . . . maybe we should have overlooked them with more energy and discipline and just realized that there's no perfect place anywhere in the world. That's it!

Perhaps we should have stayed put and been more tolerable with the snowbirds, more patient with the increased crowds, more acceptable of Red Tide and the myriad of other distractions that made us dissatisfied.

If that's all true, then, we have good reason to want to return to our nice little house that won't sell and the beaches and flowers and natural beauty everywhere, especially on our back porch.

Am I really as messed up as I sound? It's like I haven't learned a single thing and I'm back to square one. Is that possible? Here I am making all these excuses for what we did. And we've barely given St. Louis a chance to make things right by us.

Well, today was the day. It was an unusually bright, sunny Sunday and we had a bad case of cabin fever. One of our sons had taken me to a delightful butcher shop in the heart of the city and Ginny couldn't join us that day. So I owed it to her to take her for a shopping experience like didn't exist anywhere in Florida. It was a unique place with specialties from all parts of *The Continent.*

Getting there, however, posed a slight problem. I couldn't get hold of any of the kids for directions so I left our house less than certain that I could retrace David's route to the store. Oh how wrong I was. Fortunately, I landed about a mile from the place and after following a rather circuitous route, Ginny got us to the door via her cell phone. Lost a lot of time, but she was delighted to find "The Butcher Shop" after a bit of unintended sightseeing.

We bought a minimal first-visit bag of meats, agreeing to wait until the next time to stock-up when we were in a more adventurous mood. We headed back for our apartment which was quite a long way from the shop.

Once again, I made the mistake of believing I knew my way around. From the shop, I figured I'd head south toward the downtown area. Boy, did I get us lost, I mean, *really* lost, not *dangerously* but close to it.

I saw the landmark *Gateway Arch* not too far ahead and knew if I could pass it, I could get back on a road that headed west. A wrong turn, a very risky U-turn, and a bit of fear took us through several neighborhoods where only Law Officers would dare to venture.

Ginny warned, "This is the area where all the shootings take place. Just yesterday, there were four killings at that intersection we just passed. Did you know that? Do you know where you are?"

No, I didn't. Not a clue, only that I was headed north when I should have been headed west. My dashboard compass told me that much. Thank the Lord that our guardian angel was on board.

This is an appropriate time to mention a terrible segment of the history of St. Louis, one that is contrary to my positive thoughts about the region.

On August 9, 2014, Michael Brown Jr., an 18-year-old African American man, was fatally shot by 28-year-old police officer Darren Wilson in the city of Ferguson, Missouri, a suburb of St. Louis. Protests immediately roiled the streets, businesses burned, and daily violence drew national and international attention.

Missouri Governor Jay Nixon appointed a blue-collar task force, the Ferguson Commission. It identified 47 urgent calls to action in four broad categories: criminal justice, youth, racial equity, and economic opportunity.

Now, five years later, those tasked with continuing the commission's work say just five *calls* have been achieved. This week, the St Louis Post-Dispatch examines an aspect of each of the Commission's broad priorities.

The first day focuses on black mothers and babies that are still dying at alarming rates while one black woman works for just pennies in change.

Also, the municipal justice system sees fewer abuses but wonders if reform will last much longer. Racial disparities in income and poverty remain stark as segregation continues to make it worse.

So at this writing, the city of Ferguson still faces enormous challenges while remaining hopeful that more corrections will take place in the near future. In Ferguson, there is still hope as the residents of the city of St. Louis continue to support the brave people of its beleaguered neighbor.

At this moment, I'm driving quite a distance from that suburb and I still worry about violence and danger lurking just outside our vehicle. We are aware of that but continue to be lost in the city!

After passing the famed Anheuser-Busch brewery a number of times, we get ourselves back in the right direction. And after all that, we drive by the Butcher Shop again. Yes, we had been driving in circles, until I figured it out. Eventually, we arrived home safely, and a lot more knowledgeable about the roadmap of St. Louis. Getting lost in the city would not happen again. It wasn't healthy.

I'm continually amazed at what a *large* city St. Louis appears to be, I mean, in terms of the geography within its boundaries, and then including the suburbs. The latest population figures list just over 300,000 people in the city, making it the 58th most populous city in America. In 1960, however, it was the 9th largest metro area. So the population has, indeed, been shrinking. The total count for the metro area is now almost three million, including all of the suburbs. Enough about geography. Let's return to the story of *A Moving Experience.*

On a very different note. This one is more personal than I've gotten in this book, so I ask for understanding. I'll protect the identity of one of our children because not only isn't it important but he deserves to have his privacy.

Just prior to our accepting this challenge of the move, we learned that one of our sons had been diagnosed with prostate cancer. It hadn't spread and surgery was the recommended solution. The timing was impeccably perfect and the hand that scheduled it was unquestionably merciful and divine.

If you'll recall, we arrived in St. Louis on March 8th. His surgery had been planned for March 27th, the date of my 84th birthday. So we were moved in (barely) and right up the street from the hospital where the surgery was to take place. Ginny and I were present at the hospital along with our son's wife. We greatly appreciated being there.

When we saw our son being wheeled from the operating room to his regular bed, his first words to me were, "Happy Birthday!" It meant a lot and we encouraged his recovery with frequent visits.

Merely one month after the surgery, routine tests indicated the lingering presence of cancer cells. That fact didn't panic the medical team but certainly got his attention. As we stand now, the cancer patient will require brief treatments of radiation therapy until the small trace of the disease is gone. To say the least, it's worrisome news at a time when it wasn't expected. And that kind of negative news is never welcome.

CHAPTER FOURTEEN

Searching

I've only briefly mentioned our son, John, the man who is currently institutionalized nearby with serious mental deficiencies. I'll mention him again because he is so special and certainly one of the reasons we moved back to St. Louis.

There was a time, when John was only 6 years old, that we faced the difficult decision to place him in a school where he could receive better care. Additionally, it would provide the rest of the family with a more normal way of life. We were living in a Dallas suburb at the time and were able to place him in The Denton State School just outside of Dallas.

We thought we were ready for his placement outside our home, but we realized on the day we left him at Denton, that the anguish of "goodbye" was the greatest and deepest pain we would ever experience in all of our years as parents. That is not an overstatement!

We left John with capable members of the staff, gave him many hugs and kisses, and walked from the building where he would live his new life. By the time we arrived at our car, both Ginny and I were blotting tears from our eyes. Then, as we exited the grounds of the

State School, our cheeks flooded with a downpour like never before. I recall being forced to pull onto a grassy border alongside the road before entering the Interstate.

Ginny and I held and squeezed each other for a long time. We wiped tears from each other's eyes. Our chests and bodies heaved with spasms. It was, indeed, the first time we felt physical pain from emotional trauma. Our hearts were broken, paining as one but splitting as suffering individual parents.

We had experienced the inexpressible sorrow of separation. There was an emptiness in our hearts. The void was never to be filled. John would forever belong to someone else.

Perhaps much of the empty space was consumed by the harsh realization that John would never again live under the same roof with his family. He would forever be a *guest* in his own home and his young siblings would have a struggle accepting him as one of them.

Ginny and I concluded that we loved John as much as any of the other children, not *more*, not *less*, but equally. But the connection was clear: by loving all of the children so much, we had made a difficult decision that would benefit all of them. And it was conclusive!

To place him at the State School was made easier by the fact that we had no choice. John needed and deserved special care to help him live an essential life, and the other children needed and deserved a lifestyle that was conducive to healthy learning and development.

It could be said that there was really no decision at all. It was so obviously the correct choice for John and for all of us as a family. Denton would be a sanctuary where John would find greater peace. At the same time, there was the opportunity to continue exploring his mind.

Later on, when we relocated to St. Louis for the first time, John was accepted at a State School where he has lived for over 55 years of his life as he approaches his 62nd birthday.

Throughout this *Moving Experience*, I've taken you along on a search for the most dramatic sign that we've done the right thing in moving back to St. Louis. It's been an arduous trek but I think we're getting closer. I keep waiting for bells to ring, for a loud fanfare signaling, "This is it!" But so far, I haven't yet heard that.

Up to this point, it's been more like an accumulation of many signs that are a source for confidence, a step toward declaring that the bells have been ringing ever since we moved into our apartment from Florida.

But now, after adding a bit about John's home here in St. Louis, that's certainly one of the factors that weighs heavily in favor of the move. We're much more at ease knowing that he's close by.

I've concluded, too, that there just might not be a loud ringing of bells to signal "Good Move!" The *peace of mind* might be enough, a lot more subtle than applause and brash music. More like a quiet passage from a Beethoven Symphony.

From our very first thought that the move was the right thing to do, we both felt we heard a voice advising us. There was never a doubt about that. We heard a voice counseling us. Our faith supports the idea that it is a Holy Spirit Who counsels and recommends such things, God Himself calling us to inspirational, intellectual action. So we digest it all and pray that the meal satisfies our hunger for affirmation of our plan.

Just when I don't need an opposing force tugging at me, the local newspaper, The St. Louis Post-Dispatch, runs an article in the weekend travel section on Sanibel Island and Captiva, two shining gems of Florida Gulf Coast beauty.

The article stirs such deep memories that I'm obliged to pursue another *"slip"* to Sanibel. I knew it was my inability to perceive changes in St. Louis that had occurred over time on things that I thought should have remained static and permanent. And the way to accept them was to *slip* back to Florida. Figure that out. But it always worked.

The news article promoted the popular magnet that draws the most tourists to the area, the incredible natural accumulation of seashells on the Sanibel sands. It's what first drew us to that place over 40 years ago.

Washing the shells are the purest waters and softest sand beaches you'll find anywhere. All along the shoreline are indigenous seagulls that circle the air and walk the sands in search of microscopic prey. They chatter loudly and animate the sky overhead with their noisy conversations.

Further along the beach, Sanibel joins Captiva at *Blind Pass* where a small bridge of water between them was hewn by a decades-old hurricane. It's a smooth transition from one island to the next. The quiet road is covered by giant palms, hibiscus, and bougainvillea that resemble trees more than bushes as they join across the top and shape a canopy.

I could go on and on and fill many pages with praise for those two small islands. But I'm already sounding far too much like the Public Relations and Tourism departments for these places when they really don't need that at all. I'll return to St. Louis.

My brief imagination exercise offered only momentary relief from the spring rain and chilling temperatures embracing St. Louis. It's not easy being cold and wet versus warm and dry, especially while "picking up some rays" along the way.

I'm reminded always that this *Moving Experience* has been hard work, because it's encompassed so many elements that are difficult to control, things like ideas, attitudes and desires. We've encountered every one of them at almost every level of the process, at times moving ahead but at other times taking backward steps in a direction opposite of where we want to go.

The basic lesson Ginny and I have learned is that we can't force things to happen, whether they're physical things or things like feelings and judgments of new surroundings and new people. It seems we're constantly tested and quizzed. And that keeps us taught and stressed. I think we have a tendency to want things to be different from the way they are right now. It's a part of our human nature. And we've been no different from those around us, old friends and new who surround us.

Once again we ask, "Why did we elect to do this in the first place? Was it just a whim, a product of boredom and aging? Or was it as we've said, to benefit our children and ourselves.

As you've read along, I assume you're developing an opinion of your own based on our changing moods. I suppose (hope) you're hearing us on the positive side. We're doing more things we *like* to do rather than the opposite. And that's what this is all about. We certainly haven't accepted the challenges because we're masochistic and enjoy punishing ourselves.

If we were both pushed to give an honest answer right now as to how we feel about the move, we'd have to say we're at the 50/50 point. We're pretty sure we like what we've done, but then again, we have a few doubts that we haven't yet cultivated enough trust in ourselves to claim victory.

By now, we've meekly recognized that we cannot go back to Florida and call it "home." We're far beyond that and we could never convince ourselves that we've yet tried hard enough. So we proceed with diligence, commitment, and a level of fervor we haven't quite reached . . . onward and upward to the finish line. It's the perseverance and the persistence of an Olympian that we strive for. Nothing else will do.

I was just thinking about my own history and I figured that maybe this wanderlust to relocate and to take risks might be in my blood. I think, "The apple didn't fall far from the tree."

My Father was born in a small village outside of Vienna, Austria, back in 1901. When he was just 19 years old, he left alone for America. He was the oldest of nine children and his father had recently passed away. He was the sole means to support his mother and the children.

So he ventured out, with no knowledge of the English language and a few distant relatives at his destination of Chicago. He soon met my Mom and they lived in a happy marriage for over 50 years.

When they were both approaching their 80's and 90's, their health was affecting their ability to get around and to care for their own medical needs. So we invited them to move to St. Louis to be closer to us. I was an only child and they were happy to bring themselves closer to us and their seven grandchildren. Does the scenario sound familiar?

Yes, they relocated to be nearer to their child and grandchildren. And they moved close to us in Ballwin, Missouri, in the same apartment complex where Ginny and I now reside. (I forgot to mention that Dan and I also had our office in this complex. And so did our youngest son, Frank, in his College years. Coincidence? There just might be some other force at play here.)

So what Ginny and I chose to do wasn't such a unique or heroic idea after all. Lots of people do it. And lots make their offsprings and themselves happier for it. After all, it's a big, wide, wonderful world out there and it's almost a pity to remain in one place for all of one's life.

Sometimes, it takes a while to find a place to live life in true joy, in the *heart* as well as in the *home*. In *this* place, we've found that we're better connected to our true nature. We've discovered the roots of genuine humor and we find ourselves laughing more than ever . . . in boundless joy.

So what does that say about our move from Florida? First of all, it again confirms our decision. We've done the right thing, even though it's gotten plenty rough from time to time. But we've just about arrived at the point where we're ready to hear those bells ringing out in a loud salute to our mettle and our mindset.

For sure, we'll be more secure when we sell our house in Fort Myers. But right now, we move through our days knowing that we're safe and that nothing can harm us because we're surrounded by so many members of a loving family.

Among our other achievements, we've learned that when you get right down to it, one city is about the same as another. Except, maybe, for the climate. Even then, you can live within *any* climate because you spend most of your time inside anyway. So you *can* grow accustomed to the outside and just stop grousing. Nobody wants to hear you anyway. So you accept the climate and make the best of it. That's a lot smarter than fighting it.

I had a recent phone conversation with a good friend in Fort Myers. We exchanged many stories, especially his to me about how nice it was down there, "Many fewer autos since the snowbirds have gone back up north," he said proudly.

But he also said something that made me happy not to be there . . . the temperature was back to summer highs in the upper nineties.

Honestly, that was not pleasant weather. Good for one thing only, submersing the body in cool water, a pool.

So the "climate change," the difference between the two locations that I've talked about?

On second thought, we've figured that it really isn't that important after all. Yeah, it's nice in the winter when there's snow falling up here, but it doesn't last for a long time, perhaps a couple of months. (Do you see how one can justify a decision by simply changing perspective . . . and attitude. Human moods are as mercurial as the weather.)

CHAPTER FIFTEEN

Making Small Talk

Ginny and I agree that it's about time for one of our late-night talks at the kitchen table, the ones that involve candlelight and tea. There's an awful lot of stuff that deserves discussion while surrounded by tranquility and love. So we selected a night when we were not overtired. We began around 9:00pm, eager to share opinions. The candle was loaded with a long wick and the pot was brimming with hot tea.

Ginny began: "Are you prepared to admit defeat?" she began. "*You've* been the one who's hung on the longest. But you appear much happier now than I've seen you in a long time. Right?"

"Of course, you're right, my dear. You've always been able to read me perfectly."

"This one has taken a lot longer than usual."

"I just loved it so much in Florida and it's taken me awhile to get accustomed to these differences."

"What's been your biggest hang-up?"

"I think just *everything* . . . the people have been the easiest to adjust to, very kind and friendly people up here. But I guess the poor weather season we've encountered here has made it awful difficult.

Just nothing like it is in Florida, even though I know it's getting quite hot down there."

"What else?" she asked.

"I don't really think it helps to list the negatives right now since I've overcome them and adjusted well in the past month."

"So you don't want to make any confessions about your behavior, your cranky moods that began almost every day."

"Nope! I think it's very counterproductive to talk about those things. Do you want an apology?"

"It would be nice," she answered. "You've been a bit hard to live with."

"All right, then. I'm very sorry. Sorry I hurt you and made life difficult. Does that help?"

"Of course, it does," she said as she reached over and squeezed my hand. I squeezed back and smiled. It was nice to be in complete agreement again after struggling to be our usually compatible selves. It meant all the difference in the world.

"Are you feeling better, now?" I asked. "Or do you want me to list all the barriers I've knocked aside to be content with this place?"

"It would be nice. But it's not necessary."

"Okay, then, I won't go through all the trouble. I still think it's counterproductive to go backwards now that we've reached our conclusion."

"I've got to make one complaint before we end this discussion, my dear," Ginny said firmly. "It's about those "*slips*" you were having, those times when you went off to a netherworld somewhere and I couldn't reach you, until you were ready."

"Those bothered you?" I asked gently.

"Of course, they did. They didn't really make me angry because I knew you needed that. But it was getting a little old."

"I feel one coming on right now, since you mentioned it."

"Darling, please." She sounded pitiful as she pleaded with me.

"C'mon. Let me help you remember," I said. "How about those trips we took up to Sarasota. Man, I love that city. Always wished we could've lived there. Beautiful place."

"I concur. It's a wonderful place. But it *was* a tedious two-hour drive from our house to Saint Armand Circle . . . to *Columbia Restaurant.*"

"You remember what I used to say each time we arrived there and we were seated?"

"How could I forget," Ginny answered back. "You always said, 'there's nowhere in the world I'd rather be right now.' And I always agreed."

"Driving there wasn't too shabby either," I said. "I loved driving alongside the Gulf, over Siesta Key and all those million-dollar homes. Remember how we used to point out the winter home of Stephen King? It was shaped like a boat."

"And beyond Siesta, after lunch, we'd sometimes drive up and around Anna Maria Island."

"That was the ultimate in peace and quiet. Not many cars, blue Gulf waters right beside the road, and we'd stop for ice cream at the tip of the Island. I remember . . . those were some great times. But the four-hour drive up there and back was beginning to get to us. Both of our backs bothered us and we walked around like cripples for a couple of days. Remember that, too?"

"It's still a place of dreams. And you didn't seem to mind shopping those elegant stores."

"Never brought much home from there," Ginny said quickly. "It was far too expensive. You ready to come back to reality now?"

"I think I am, yes."

"Nothing wrong with reliving such happy moments, my dear," Ginny said. "Nothing wrong with that at all. I hope you'll be able to amass many such times in our lives up here."

"I've already accumulated tons of excellent memories here, with and without the kids. I know that'll continue as long as our health holds out."

"I've got a question for *you* this time," I asked with high confidence. "Do you miss your favorite Doctor? She was so good for you and always seemed very interested in helping you."

"She *was* very good *for* me and *to* me," Ginny responded. "Yes, I do miss her very much and it was a long way to drive to see her on Marco Island, but the hour and a half was worth it. To clarify my answer, yes, I do miss her. But I'm sure I'll find another good Physician up here before long."

"One more thing," I leaned back on my chair and winced a little, not wanting to hurt her feelings but curious and caring enough to solicit an honest reply. "How about your friends?" I asked. "I know you miss the closest ones, like Barbara and Audrey and Carly. But how much? You seem to be getting along okay without them. But does it sadden you to be so far away. I mean, they must need you just as much as you need them."

"I've learned to live without them," she said. "But to answer your question, yes, I certainly do miss them, a lot."

I detected a tear in one of Ginny's eyes and regretted having asked the blunt question. I gently wiped the tear and apologized for being so insensitive. We both shifted in our chairs and simultaneously rose to stretch.

I asked a lovely, tiring lady if she was getting sleepy and wanted to stop our dialogue. She shook her head and silently mimed the words, "Not in the least. I can out-last you any time. You know how

I enjoy doing this. Just you and me and nobody else but this candle and hot tea in the whole world."

"What do you think is happening to this place, I mean, our world," Ginny asked quizzically. "So many good people we knew all our life are passing away, and we're left behind. Just yesterday, Doris Day died at the age of 97 . . . and today, another favorite of ours, Tim Conway, died at 85. It's kind of scary, isn't it? I think our number's around he corner. What do you think?"

"You really can't say that, my love. We know that we're going to die and we've talked a lot about it as the years have passed. But neither of us is particularly frightened at the prospect. I think we're both ready to meet our Maker whenever He's ready for us. No fear, no anxiety, no turning Him down."

"And I also feel much better now that we've decided our final resting place will be here in St. Louis, right up the street at St. Joseph Cemetery."

"Good point, my dear. It was a good decision." Ginny appeared refreshed and ready to leave this topic and move on to something else. So I brought up a thought I'd been carrying for some time. It was my own recognition of the fact that I was being terribly *judgmental* through the entire process of selecting one geography over another, Sanibel versus St. Louis." At that moment, I "judged" that a confession was in order. So I began:

"You know," I said, "it's occurred to me that I was acting very irrationally. I mean, who am I, really, to be *judging* everyone and everything connected to this move? Who am I to be calling everybody out and determining who's good and who's bad, who's right and who's wrong. Isn't that the way I've been acting . . . *judging?*"

"I don't know if you could actually call it *judging.* I've thought all along that you're just moving from suffering to elation. And you haven't been able to make an accurate discernment yet."

"I know you've quietly listened to me through it all. And you've probably formed your own ideas. By now, you must've formed the opinion that I have such definite ideas and opinions about *everything* that I'm bordering on playing God."

"You *have* been opinionated, my dear."

"Thank you," I said, "You're being very kind. I've heard myself over and over again, 'I like this and I don't like that . . . over and over . . . it's been so black and white.' I've been making judgments based on *my* discernment and only mine. I've been judging quality through my eyes only and nobody else's. That's clearly *not* who I want to be."

"Well, you've taken the first step in leaving that part of you behind and starting anew. It's an unhealthy state of mind and it's been consuming you. I know it's because you've been fighting a lot of demons that won't go away. They're against the very fiber of whom and what you are in your own mind, how you want *yourself* to behave.

"For the most part, I've left you alone," Ginny continued. "In cases like this, you usually find your own answer, come to your own conclusions without my help. And that's what's been happening right here, tonight."

As always, Ginny was able to see through my façade and totally understand where I'm coming from. What an absolute gem she is.

She waited a minute and then asked, "Is there such a word as judgmentation, or judgmentalism? Is that what your malady is called?"

My only answer was a smile, almost a laugh, and a jerk of my head backwards. "Maybe there aren't such words, my dear, but there ought to be. It's an ailment that's sweeping society, sweeping the world right now. Everybody has an answer for the ills of others . . . we're all obsessed with the *judgment* thing. I'd call it an illness."

"Maybe you and me can start a trend," Ginny said. "Maybe we can spread a sort-of plague around the world and get people to stop judging others. Imagine a world without that insidious illness. Wouldn't it be nice? I'll bet just you and me could start a trend if we'd stick to an opposite practice. So what would be the opposite of being judgmental?"

I had to think about that one for a minute, finally uttering something not so wise, "Hmm, the opposite of judgmental. Maybe it's *non-judgmental.* That's the best I can do right now. But there might be something else floating around out there.

"I'd bet that one-half of all the judgments over all the earth are incorrect," I said. "Why, even at the top, you know how many legal cases they're overturning these days where an individual was inaccurately and unjustly incarcerated for years and then found to be innocent. That's one of the worst mistakes in the world and it's done every day through our own democratic judicial system."

"In my case, I can't even count how many single items I've been wrong about in my judgments about St. Louis."

"Like, name a few, my dear." I had hoped that Ginny wouldn't take me literally, but she was insistent in her request for a list of things I've recently been wrong about.

Not easy to enumerate, and I really don't take kindly to admitting each and every one of them. So I finally just figured, "Well, I'm sure she won't spread my sins throughout our family and all over the community."

She isn't like that, so I'm probably safe in thinking she'll protect me. The heading will be something like, "*The items and the people I've misjudged while making my decision about St. Louis versus Sanibel.*" That sounded silly enough so that nobody could possibly take me seriously.

CHAPTER SIXTEEN

Is This the End?

"Starting out, I do recall getting so angry with the people at the Department of Motor Vehicles for making me endure great agony over a period of weeks. I thought the whole bunch was ignorant and mean-spirited. That was inaccuracy number one! I later met a neighbor of ours who worked there and she was very bright and kind, thereby belying my initial opinion.

"Then there was the weather," I continued. "I figured that the daily forecast was a conspiracy among local meteorologists to make me irritable and despondent. But then I learned that one of the TV weather ladies attended our church and turned out to be an unusually pleasant and patient woman.

"Now, I can't go on like this for the hundred or so items that made me look foolish," I said. "But I think you get the idea. It covered people, places and things, all items in which I changed my mind because I learned the truth was different from my initial opinion. The embarrassing result was inaccurate judgmental behavior!"

"How about all the times I left friends hanging in suspense while I went off on my tangential mental soirees back to Florida. How about all of those? Even best friends were writing me off as being a little off my rocker."

Enough of that! Ginny was happy and proud that I was man enough to admit my failings. Besides, it taught me a lesson about being so blind that I believed I was flawless. Never again!

Before we closed the evening, there was one lingering question that I still had for Ginny. I was curious to find out what she didn't like about Florida, I mean, the big stuff. So I asked.

"It wasn't so much what I *didn't* like," she said, it was those intangibles in our lifestyle that I had trouble coping with."

"Like what, for example?" I asked.

"Like the terribly hot summers," was a quick reply. "They were just awful. I couldn't even go outside, could never even think about having a garden because nothing would grow in the sandy soil under that blazing sun. Do you want to hear more?" she asked with a note of sarcasm.

"If you have more, yes, I'm up to it."

"Okay, then. I'll give it to you straight. Those *snowbirds* drove me nuts. All winter long, the way they drove, the way they shoved me around in the grocery store or even in church for that matter. They were horrible and I just couldn't tolerate them, especially the visitors from New Jersey, even those from our home town of Chicago."

"So is that it?"

"Not at all, Ginny said," rather loudly. She was, indeed, getting all worked-up over this thing. I said calmly, "Okay, give me some more. But be kind."

"The greatest thorn in my side was the social climbing, not just from the people in Naples, but even those who lived next door or up the street. Everybody had to have the best or the biggest, or the most expensive car, their Maserati and their Bentley . . . it started to make me sick.

"I never dreamed that people with money, *lots* of money, could be that selfish and that competitive. I'm surprised that more people don't crack-up because of their inability to keep up with their neighbor. Even their professions. If you're not a Doctor, you'd better have some other lofty initials following your name.

"I remember encountering a lot of people who wouldn't give me the time of day because I wasn't dressed expensively, fashionably. And you know I'm just not that type. I come from humble beginnings . . . and so did you, from immigrant parents and grandparents.

"The bottom line, in that area of America, you and me, we just didn't fit in. We were incompatible with the people who lived down there, either as snowbirds or as vacationers, or as natives."

"Wow . . . you're really fired up about this, aren't you, my dear. Calm down. Take it easy. You're not there any more. You're in St. Louis where we both fit in very comfortably."

The strangest thing happened after Ginny and I moved toward our bedroom to call it a night. It had to be a good omen. We stopped at the patio door and opened it to breathe some clear, fresh, nighttime air. I froze in my tracks to see way above my head, a gorgeous full moon. It was spectacular, the very first full moon we had seen in St. Louis since we came here several months ago. Either we were in bed when there were other full moons. Or we just failed to notice it because we went to bed early. . . or we never looked up.

Anyway, our interpretation was, it was a good omen. There's an old superstition that says when there's a full moon a person should start a new job or finish old business. We took it to mean for us, to finish old business.

The past days and nights had ended and I was ready to move forward with a healthier, happier attitude and a new life. Ginny was ready, too. If only we could sell that house in Fort Myers!

In the meantime, Ginny is absolutely indefatigable. There is no end to her energy and her passion to make our apartment "home." Even though she spends a lot of time in the basement, that also is a sizeable (and frustrating) part of *home.* For it's there that she sorts the contents of those still-loaded boxes . . . sorts, divides, relocates, empties, etc. It's an enormous job that no one else is willing to tackle. So all of us remain in gratitude for her spirit of volunteerism.

A happy day! Our granddaughter, Abby, is celebrating her fifteenth birthday today and it's the first time we've lived here to celebrate it with her. She's an only child and incredibly happy because we're here. She's the daughter of our son, David, and his wife Jenny. Because she's been such an important part of our move, I've got to mention a little about her.

Ginny and I have been blessed with seven great children and seven grand children. Of the latter, Abby is one of only three girls and she's about the prettiest thing you've ever seen.

Like most kids her age, she exudes energy. She talks fast, thinks faster, and moves like a rabbit. But beneath her blurred actions, Abby is capable of profound reasoning.

My personal friendship with her began when she was six years old. We were living in Florida at the time, but it didn't stop Abby from getting to know me and me her. Her secret was the telephone. She called me at least twice a week. The conversations could last an hour, most times about half that, and occasionally five or ten minutes.

I remember, each time I heard her birdlike voice on the phone, my heart soared and my blood pressure plunged. For Abby's voice dripped with sincerity and honesty. And from that sprung endless happiness. When our conversations ended, we generally wiped away a tear or two from our eyes with a short "love you" from each of us.

Perhaps the sugery peace in Abby's heart is so refreshing because it's loaded with so much love. That's how she's been able to wrap an 84-year old grandpa around her finger and bestow on him the endowment of perpetual peace. She continues to be one of the great benefits of our move back to St. Louis. And so I make a special remark: "Happy 15th Birthday, Abby."

CHAPTER SEVENTEEN

More Stories

"Bear with me for one last reminder of Florida, my dear," I said to Ginny. "I'm sure you'll enjoy recalling this trip with me. It's unforgettable."

"Remember visiting that quiet, restful, little village called Key West." I said that with a tone of sarcasm because anyone who's been there knows it's anything but 'quiet and restful.'"

"Ah, Key West," Ginny said in reply. "Key West. After just a short time in Florida, we were smitten with pictures of the place. And your worship of Jimmy Buffet. You liked him a lot."

"I do recall the story you want to relive," Ginny continued. "And I'm honestly not too eager to do it. It's not a pleasant memory."

"Oh, c'mon," I said to her. "Let's not get so serious. Let's have a little fun." I was happy she allowed me to continue because, on reflecting, we thought it was one of the most hilarious adventures we ever had in the entire state of Florida.

"Okay," I began. "So the plan was to drive over the keys right into Key West, down at the very tip of the island chain. So the car we had at the time was the Chrysler PT Cruiser. You always thought they were so 'cute.'

"So we were heading across Alligator Alley around 9:30 in the morning, driving about 65-70 miles an hour. And all of a sudden, we hear this *bang,* and with it, there's a spray of water all over the windshield. The radiator blew! Water sprayed from the broken hoses and from holes in the radiator itself. It didn't take a rocket scientist to figure out that the engine sort-of *exploded!*

"From your recollections, you know we had never experienced anything like it in our lives. Alligator Alley was pretty much in the dark since the sun hadn't fully risen. It was just peeking its head up from the horizon in front of us.

"So we knew that the car couldn't be driven. We put the hood up and waited, hopefully for a Florida State Trooper to come along and help us get towed to Fort Lauderdale because we were closer to that coast than to the Gulf."

"I knew you were dreaming because we never had luck like that," Ginny said. "You might also recall, my dear, that in those days, cell phones didn't exist so we were at the mercy of the State of Florida. And as the sun rose, it started to get *hot.* That was my first experience with real Florida *hot.*

"So here we are, standing beside the car with the four doors open and insects beginning to hover around us. And I mean *insects . . .* remember? We were standing on the shoulder of the road in the *everglades,* one of the most hostile environments in the entire world.

"There were *thousands* of mosquitoes buzzing around our ears and eyes, *flies* in every color of the rainbow, *stinging bugs* like wasps and hornets, and there was a small creek behind us, flowing parallel to our car, undoubtedly teaming with alligators and snakes. Of course, with our doors open, all of these creatures had access to the *inside*. And as you were prone to say, 'we were getting eaten alive.'

"Finally, after an hour of growing anxiety and fear, an officer stops to give us help. And we were like, 'Eureka!' We've been saved. The officer told us he'd radio ahead and have a tow truck get us.

"Well, my dear, you remember that another hour passed as we watched dozens of cars wave to us without stopping. Finally, some kind stranger stopped. He had a few bags of water he donated to pour over and into the engine to cool it down. It did that but did nothing to get the car started. We did, nevertheless, we have high hopes that the stranger would at least get someone to save us from an ignominious death."

Ginny quivered from time to time thinking out loud about the insects and snakes. She wasn't exactly the everglades-explorer type and waited eagerly for the story to reach its conclusion, sooner rather than later.

"Needless to say, both of us were getting a little frustrated to see so many cars flying past us. After still another hour, a driver with a tow truck stopped and hooked us up to his vehicle. Obviously, we needed a different vehicle, one that could get us to Key West. He dropped us off at a dealer in Fort Lauderdale and the only vehicle he had was a truck, a *Chevy Silverado*, a very *large* vehicle."

Ginny began laughing and commented, "I had never seen anything quite that silly in all my life, the sight of you and me in that truck. And we're both fairly small people. This thing had a back seat that was like a sleeper, with a bed above the seat."

"So we signed the papers and were off to the Keys, looking terribly out-of-place high above the pavement in our Silverado. But at least we were safe and out of traffic as well as the multi-colored creatures of the Everglades.

"We were a rather formidable sight driving around the small, narrow streets of Key West in this giant vehicle and once, in parking at the Hyatt Hotel, you remember how we got trapped in such a small slot that we couldn't leave until two other cars decided to depart.

"It was truly a hellacious experience. After two days, we had seen enough of Key West. But it gave us an extraordinary story to tell relatives and friends, a bitter taste of Florida neither one of us would forget."

CHAPTER EIGHTEEN

Comparisons

"So that's how we began our life in Florida. Let me recall a much better recollection of how we just began our second time around here in St. Louis. It was at the time when I was still resisting everything about this place and you suggested we go down to the Climatron, remember?"

"Of course, I was praying you'd like it."

"Well, we didn't get a very good parking spot so I figured the entire visit might be a bit on the negative side. But right after we went through the visitor's gate, things changed. We walked into the magnificent outdoor garden and headed for the *Climatron*, the startling geodesic dome designed by R. Buckminster Fuller. It housed the popular tropical plant collection and I knew I was going to like being in that environment again.

"Once inside, I liked it even more as we followed that winding path beside waterfalls and around exotic pools, plants and trees of every tropical variety. I've got to admit, I enjoyed every minute of that with your narrative, my dear. You seemed to be the 'know-it-all,' though you stumbled over a few horticultural facts. And I do also remember getting very hungry about that time."

"But as we approached the restaurant," Ginny recalled, "we discovered a major deterrent to our idea. You remember the long line with a few dozen people waiting to enter the restaurant? And the line was moving at a snails' pace? I remember commenting in not a very Christian fashion, 'Yeah, these old people eat so slowly, it's maddening. And I've never been one who's patient enough to wait in a long line when I'm hungry."

"So I had an alternate idea," Ginny said. "I hesitated to mention it because it was presumptuous of me. And I warned you that it revealed my passion for St. Louis hot dogs."

"Ah," I quickly responded, telling you that I *love* hot dogs, loved them all my life. That day, even the weather collaborated. The temperature reached a high of 78 degrees."

"I ordered the usual dosage of two 'dogs' for me, one for you, one small fries for both of us, and two Diet Cokes. Not the healthiest diet on earth, but it certainly didn't hurt us just that one time.

"And you recall the picnic table where that lovely family was sitting with their three children?"

"Of course, the table was under a large, a big, shady oak tree. And right when we joined them and started to eat the hot dogs, I started to laugh out loud. It was enough to startle the people around us."

"Oh, I recall all too well," Ginny commented. "I couldn't understand what caused such a loud uproar and I asked if it was something I did?"

"I hate to tell you," I said with due respect, "if you lower your chin, you'll see what's amusing me. It's unkind of me, but it's hilarious. I know that it'll make you smile. It's just hysterical!"

"So I reluctantly did as you asked and I joined you in laughter. It had been a long time since I displayed my sense-of-humor. And you, my dear, graphically described what you were looking at."

Without hesitation, you shouted, "Do you see down the front of your sweater? Do you see what I see? Look at what you've done."

"We both sat there and stared together at a stream of bright yellow mustard that was slowly trickling down from right near my chin to my waist, impolitely oozing from the hot dog bun."

"Yeah, I remember astutely grabbing several napkins and dabbing the yellow stripe. The two of us could not control ourselves. But the cause of the hilarity wasn't finished.

"Do you recall how I pointed to *your* chest? I told you to lower *your* chin just the way you had ordered me to do. And we were both driven to even *more* laughter. You remember what it looked like? Running down from *my* hot dog, in identical fashion to yours, was a straight yellow line of mustard."

"We were both so stunned that each of us nearly fell from the bench into a fresh pile of wet leaves. And I truly believe that was a turning point. I seemed to like St. Louis more from that day on. I think we were both so humbled before the other one that we lost ourselves and our inhibitions at the same time."

Ginny also reminded me of our visit to the *Butterfly House*, where we were both enchanted by the environment that was colored by over 5000 butterflies. "So you see, when combined, we found tons of interesting venues to keep us occupied."

In our earlier days in St. Louis, Ginny was known to volunteer at the *Butterfly House* and she enjoyed every minute of the time. It's an amazing place where you can watch butterflies emerge from their chrysalis and also study native and migratory species in the outdoor garden. It's a wonderful place to visit and very near to our apartment.

"There's a similar *House* in Naples, Florida, but it's not nearly as impressive as this one. (Never thought I'd talk that way about my beloved Florida compared to St. Louis.)

Well, on another subject. I thought it would never happen. We're finally digging into *The Graveyard*, that dank and dark basement underneath our apartment, that resting place of things we never should have brought back to Florida in the first place. Today's the day. It will be reckoned with.

That company I talked about earlier, *College Hunks*. Well, their slogan reads: *"Declutter Your Life with the Help of Some College Hunks."* With that sort of advertising, I questioned their reliability.

Buy hey, they've completed the job. No reason to worry. Ginny and I were delighted with the service and professionalism. They were prompt, efficient, polite, and well trained as they performed minor miracles in the basement and the garage. It now looks so much better around those spots with that important element of *trust* paying off big time.

So these two young guys appeared at the time promised and vowed to responsibly dispose of all unwanted clutter. And that they did, hauling off dozens of movers' boxes and a couple of furniture pieces that nobody wanted. I couldn't explain the glee at seeing them haul off some of those major boxes that were instrumental in making us seriously depressed. But now, we have a reasonably priced outlet that can help us transform that *Graveyard* back into a legitimate place for storage. For sure, the *College Hunks* will be called back again.

And on another subject . . . for many decades since the turn of the century, St. Louis has fostered a reputation as being one of the greatest sports cities in America. In baseball, for instance, the St. Louis Cardinals have had the most visits to a *World Series* and the most victories in a Series second only to the New York Yankees.

They welcomed the St. Louis Rams to the city, won a *Super Bowl* and were proud of their two visits to that NFL venue in three years. They then moved to Los Angeles.

In hockey, they waited a long time to revisit the *Stanley Cup Playoffs*, their only appearance being in 1970 when they lost the Championship. But right now, in the year we moved back to St. Louis, they won their Divisional Championship and will play the Boston Bruins for the Stanley Cup.

The city is glowing brightly over that accomplishment and, of course, Ginny and I are taking full credit for their championship season. Most certainly, we brought them good luck by our presence here.

I dare not compare our new city to the city of Fort Myers in its sports interest but . . . the Floridians are home to baseball's *Spring Training* for the Minnesota Twins and the Boston Red Sox. Both are formidable teams, mind you, but it's only *Spring Training*, not the Major Leagues.

So you see, we do have some pride in St. Louis, especially since we raised seven children in the shadow of The Gateway Arch. We always said, "St. Louis is a good place to raise kids." And it was.

It never faced the enormous challenges of Chicago to the north, nor the crises of New York City to the east. It was somewhere in-between, in size and in just about everything else.

The city claims its roots in history and in excellent educational facilities. It also holds its own in the world of entertainment, being a stopover for some of the biggest acts in show business. When Ginny and I think back over the years of providing for our children in this town, we recall many great shows we all saw together.

At Busch Stadium, I already mentioned the great years when the Cardinals ruled the National League in baseball and the city wasn't far behind in other major sports. We attended our share of games.

The Muny Opera, the *outdoor* concert venue, had wonderful appeal to all the population with its presentations of a variety of Broadway Musicals.

Another home of concerts was initially called the *St. Louis Arena*, and later, the *Checkerdome*. It was once the second largest such stadium in America, second only to Madison Square Garden. Ginny and I enjoyed taking our teenagers there for their introduction to many of the country's top musical stars. Or was it the other way around?

I recall seeing, among others, Elton John, Fleetwood Mack, Dolly Parton, Neal Diamond, The Who, Kenny Rogers, and even Luciano Pavarotti, and additional classical performers in his category.

Then there was and still is the great Fox Theatre, one of the most stunningly beautiful indoor theatres in all America. Better known as *"The Fabulous Fox,"* it's another Broadway venue that prides itself on a magnificent stage and an ambience unique to the nation's live performance scene. Long ago, we witnessed the performances of Michael Flatly in Riverdance, Donny Osmond in "Joseph and the Amazing Technicolor Dreamcoat," and many classical concert artists, both old and new.

There's also Powell Symphony Hall, home to The St. Louis Symphony Orchestra and almost all of the classical favorites, with notable and frequent guests like Yo-Yo Ma.

Given the chance, I could list many such concert halls, both indoor and outdoor, that comprise the music/entertainment offerings of St. Louis. But I don't want this to sound like a commercial so I'll leave my summation alone and move on to other things that attracted us to the city.

St. Louis University is a prominent Jesuit school of higher education from which four of our seven children graduated. Some studied elective courses at Washington University and another higher learning institution, Webster College.

So you can understand why we were attracted to St. Louis in the first place. Education was one of the highest goals in our role as parents and the city is loaded with opportunities and choices, both in Private and Public education. And we're proud of every one of our kids, achieving goals beyond our expectations.

CHAPTER NINETEEN

Learning the Hard Way

Here I go again. Whether you want to or not, I've got to share this with you. Right now, I'm having one of those *slips*. I'm yearning to smell the odor of saltwater and hear the sound of gulls and dolphin within the reach of my senses. And I think you're ready for it, too. So bear with me and enjoy.

I never said this choice of where to live would be easy. I talked a lot about the entertainment in St. Louis. Fort Myers has all that, too, perhaps on a smaller scale, but it's all still there.

Most of it's tucked into tiny corners of small towns. And most of the entertainers are vintage country-western stars, with names you've probably never heard. Or if you did, you haven't remembered them because it's been so long ago.

I hope you don't feel that these *slips* of mine are a waste of time. They're instinctive reactions of mind and body to stimuli through imagination. And they've been a great escape from the drudgery of a very stressful move. So allow me the pleasure of running away, at least temporarily and mentally.

There's no doubt, if you've been paying attention, you know that I'm struggling to discern clarity and vision from all of my new experiences. I want to stick to the right move and do what's best for Ginny and our family. But you can imagine how difficult it's been. I've got to get this thing right, make the correct decision for everybody's sake, the best of my friends called *family.* And also for the rest of those friends affected by my decision.

By the way, I fully realize that Ginny is in this with me. It's a joint decision we're making, let that be understood. But as the man of the house (ouch!), I feel it's my responsibility to sort-of take the lead. So, no insult intended to anyone who's offended by the way I'm running things. I don't want to lose any friends while doing this.

To be sure, *good* friends are hard to find. Across continents, into countries and communities, the search for the true "friend" is long and tedious. But once found, true friends are bound, by the special qualities of caring and love, the root and the route of friendship.

Allow yourself to walk with me on another of my *"slips,"* an imagination exercise. Test your innate ability to make friends, a.k.a. your *friendship-ability.* Lose yourself and escape to a peaceful place. Travel the *friend- ship* on a psychic journey to the edge of a calm sea. Plant yourself seaside on Captiva Island.

Imagine you're walking a lonely stretch of white sand. You're the first to pass this way this day. Your imprint sinks into the soft sand. You value this aloneness. But in the distance, a small dot grows larger. Another person is approaching. In this private place, unwanted interaction is imminent!

Like travelers in a galaxy of time, another human appears on a small piece of planet. Do you speak or remain silent? Either way, there is risk of being misunderstood, or even worse, ignored.

"Hello! Good morning." Does the greeting come easy? Does it come at all? No doubt, you'd rather not be distracted during this time of personal peace. But each of you is probably thinking: "I'm not in favor of this dalliance, but I'm obligated to speak to this other human."

Friendship-ability. It's intrinsic to more than a gregarious nature. It's the core of confidence, interest, curiosity. And Lord knows, I've been forced into learning those over the past few months.

It does seem that the person compelled to vocalize a greeting to a stranger is the one who cares more, not just about him or herself, but also about others. And usually, in the opposite order: others first, myself last, God always. Such qualities are procreators of unselfishness, the origin of peace.

As we proceed in our search for peace and patience in our own muddled minds, the intensity of our *friendship-ability* and the patience it generates are accurately measured. Occasions include but aren't limited to: retail check-out lines, queues *anywhere*, a passerby on the street, medical waiting rooms, the stranger beside us on an airline flight. Each is an opportunity for making connections with others who plead silently for the reassurance that someone in the world cares about *them.*

Peacing the world together is a common goal. But it's possible only through contact between two or more human beings . . . and a God with nothing else to do but listen.

Conversation and communication . . . they result from *friendship-ability,* the desire to reach out and *make* friends. And friends are something I've desperately missed since moving here. I had so many loyal and consistent people that I left behind in Ft Myers. Sure, I can reach a beach on my occasional *slips* into an imaginative world that provides temporary help to cure my loneliness, but it doesn't really solve problems.

Friends are what it's all about. Ginny had her own list of loyal, caring people who reached out to her many times, when she needed it most. Of course, she also loved to walk in peaceful places, but good friends helped a great deal.

And I'll tell you something else. Those quiet walks are a unique place where you can be alone to listen to your God and to hear His voice through the sounds of nature: the squeal of a gull, the wash of a wave, and the crunch of shells beneath your feet. Certainly, the Creator of such miracles uses them better than anyone else. And it's His good counsel that addresses our needs through those instruments.

Seems like we all have so many complex issues these days. It's a confusing world for Ginny and me right now. All around us, confusion reigns supreme and resists attempts to settle it.

But for us, listening to *nature* was always the best place to hear God's word. Because in that unique environment, it's always easy to hear His words skillfully translated by the gull, the wave, and the singing of shells on the shoreline. It's the kind of advice that always and quickly got my attention.

Across the St. Louis terrain and along its winding rivers, there is beauty all right. But it's less dramatic and more indirect. You can meditate on the green forests and the rippling brooks and the setting of the sun and the rising of the moon, but it's a totally different experience from walking a beach.

Remember, the title of this book includes the word "experience," explained by Webster as . . . "the practical contact with and observation of facts and events."

Well, it's been all of that. Everything, every turn of a road, every voice heard, every bird that sings, is a new and different experience for us. And at our age, *new* and *different* are not exactly the most encouraging words we want to hear. It's visibly more difficult to adapt at our stage of life than it was when we were considerably younger. But so far, we've kept our heads above water, (a pun referring to the flooding in these parts.)

Ginny and I humbly give thanks and credit to our friends in Fort Myers who have supported us through these times. They've been faithful, kind and concerned, offering their love and counsel through consistent texts, phone calls and emails. I'm reminded of a quote by my namesake, Saint Francis de Sales, who wisely predicted centuries ago, "Friendships begun in this world will be taken up again, never to be broken off." We're eager to see all of our friends again someday, but not just yet.

A new challenge has raised its head in our journey. It doesn't take a rocket scientist to figure out that the closer parents live to their children, the greater the chance for dissent and disagreement. Its almost as though vision intensifies as one grows geographically closer to ones kids.

Relationships and perceptions are duly magnified at close range. You're simply closer at hand to get involved, many times in petty issues that would dissipate if you weren't available. Small problems appear larger than they deserve to be. It's something else we've learned from moving closer to kids when you're not prepared for it, like at an older age.

So in the future, if you're inclined as we were to move closer to your kids, be certain you're up to the task. Assess the level of your tolerance, your patience, your knowledge and desire to always be available. Take it from Ginny and me, we underestimated the degree of friction that can be caused by being too close, too vulnerable.

And that can develop into a myriad of social complications. For example, there's an inclination to get involved in the personal family matters of your married children. Things like their in-laws, their medical and marital decisions, their personal challenges in raising children.

No doubt about it, when you live farther away, you aren't bothered with such daily problems, and you're much happier for it. When you're "up close and personal" to a higher degree, *their* problems can quickly become *your* problems. Under those circumstances, the dynamic within their family and your own becomes unmanageable and undesirable. Too much closeness does, indeed, breed contempt.

That's the new issue we've been facing lately. And it's not easy to cope with. In so many cases, we've appreciated the fact that the separation of hundreds and thousands of miles can sometimes reverse itself and become a good thing, a positive force rather than negative. Both sides of that conundrum surely agree that sometimes separation can be a healthy choice for parents *and* children.

We do occasionally ask ourselves, is this really what we intended by our move? Are we really helping *anyone?*

We've simplified the answer. And it goes back to the basics of *all* relationships. MYOB is how we referred to it in the old days . . . *mind your own business.* Give advice when it's requested. At other times, keep your mouth shut. Use common sense. Any one of those will do the job to provide advice and, at the same time, keep peace in the family. We have a favorite prayer in our family: "Let there be peace, at least between you and me."

You might recall that earlier in this book, like about 100 pages ago, I made a comment that stated our new commitment. The decision was, *"It's St. Louis forever!"* So it's logical to ask, "How could we possibly still be torn between Sanibel or St. Louis and be considering a move back?"

Something I want to clarify. I've always been able to differentiate between two types of *change*, the one that's inevitable in life, the kind we don't ask for, appreciate, or accept easily. It's *inevitable* change that affects nature and everything as it grows, shrinks, regenerates, reproduces, etc. It's forced upon us, cannot be stopped. So we adapt to it, sometimes kicking and screaming, but we accept it. Or we succumb to failure and submission.

Then there's the other type, the kind we initiate, create, cause. We accept it willingly because we caused it. It was deliberate and foreseen. However, because of our humanness, we have the right to . . . change our minds. And that's the clunker in the deal. We have that right to change our minds, to evaluate things differently. And that makes the experience more confusing.

We grow tired, exhausted, frustrated. Because as we continue shifting gears, we're not making progress. We may not even realize it, but we're stuck in neutral, going nowhere.

So because we caused all this in the first place, we face the cold, hard facts. We fess up. We're confronted with the need for *honesty*. If we're one of those people prone to vacillate and we change our mind excessively, then we must break loose, reach our decision, and stick with it. Even though it may include embarrassment and chagrin, it's our game to win or lose. And our spouse is in it with us. This is a partnership, remember. And we're in it together . . . forever!

CHAPTER TWENTY

Slipping in St. Louis

Today, Ginny and I, voluntarily and willingly, did something different, We foraged into the countryside of St. Louis to discover the outlying areas that comprise this part of rural Missouri. And we had a marvelous time.

First, let me tell you, we've discovered that we have a choice to make each and every day we awaken and rise from our bed. Either we succumb to laziness and hang around the house all day or we get out and explore like we did today. I'm sure you've also learned through common sense which of those is the most enjoyable. Besides, it's a joy to learn *anything* new at any time.

We saw a small ad in the newspaper this morning inviting the population to visit a unique store called *Oma's Barn*. It's a combination antique store and flower nursery charmingly tacked together inside a 125-year old red barn. Stunningly beautiful, quiet, an historic masterpiece.

Generations of the current owners have filled the barn and the acreage surrounding it for over a century. They've collected just about any artifact you can imagine. That's in addition to raising stunning flowers. Their courtesy and politeness permeates the walls and the garden of the lushly green ground.

For one thing, Ginny and I have never seen such beautiful hanging baskets anywhere, in Europe, the far East or America. Giant flowers tumble freely from the edges of huge pots, trophies created by the owners, husband and wife who are educated as professional horticulturists and whose families first inhabited this picturesque land.

Actually, the edges of the property of *Oma's Barn* rest just below a high berm that's protected them from both flood and storm for many decades. A visitor witnesses the rolling hills and valleys that have saved it from nature's wrath for so long.

As Ginny toured the outside of the Barn perusing the plants, she talked with the owner, Lisa. During that same time, I chatted inside with a male visitor and an employee. The subject was the St. Louis Blues hockey team, the one now competing for the Stanley Cup Championship.

It was one of the most stimulating, enjoyable conversations I've had in quite a while. The two strangers to one another as well as to me were so caught up in the frenzy of a World Championship that they could barely keep from stumbling over words and themselves, almost falling off their feet with enthusiasm. It was sheer joy to observe such honest energy. I actually fought back tears.

In the middle of it all, I reminded myself that I was enjoying one of those *slips* I always experience, those quick little mental journeys to fantasize about a past experience. But here I was, in the heartland of Missouri, allowing myself to appreciate the history of a beautiful, quiet landscape in the middle of America, a place as pretty as any beach I'd ever seen.

Perhaps it was the people in this country barn that delighted me the most. They were simple, polite and courteous with no false pretenses and no name-drops or mannerisms to promote their knowledge. They were just plain farmers, educated, confident and as professional as anyone you'd ever meet.

So instead of sitting around the apartment ruminating about our recent relocation problems, we had chosen to expose ourselves to refreshing new people who had quickly become friends. They were fighters not quitters, having fended off floods and stormy weather for over a century. And not about to quit any time soon.

We would visit these delightful new friends again for they taught us so much about courage, courtesy, hospitality and hard work. We had never honed those skills in nearly 20 years in Florida.

This day's experience was the first that became part of a list of fascinating places we returned to visit as time passed. Our memories were being reformed before our very eyes and in the tenderness of our hearts as we disabled the many distractions of hard times, anxiety and stress.

It's really based in love. What's love got to do with it, you ask? We believe, a lot. Because it's love that keeps Ginny and I breathing from morning 'til night. It's love that helps us appreciate new friends. And it's love that's given us the inspiration to continue our journey in spite of obstacles.

On so many occasions, we remind each other that Ginny first acquiesced almost 20 years ago to move to Florida even though she wasn't crazy about the hot summers, the mosquitoes, or the boredom of no seasonal changes. Recently, I returned the favor by agreeing to move back to St. Louis. She has been much happier since then . . . and so have I.

So, one of the many lessons we've learned from this *moving experience* is that giving of one's love to a partner is really what it's all about. It's about the *journey* not about how many times you surrender to the other's will. It's about the stops along the way that cement a marriage, the sacrifices that each makes to please the other. And it's not about keeping those occasions written in a diary, but sustaining their flow from inside your heart.

It amazes us that as the mind ages and regresses, the memories that remain the longest and the firmest are those of happy times. The times of struggle and hardship erode while the good times remain sharp and clear. Those are the ones we talk about the most.

As time went on, then, in our new home of St. Louis, we began to appreciate the little things even more. Like a stop at an ice cream stand called *Fritz's*. It's all outdoor seating and Ginny and I endured the concrete benches while we enjoyed a custard "concrete." To enhance the scene, we had invited our son, David, and his daughter, Abby.

The breeze was early spring, soft, with a temperature in the low 80's. It was a small, short pleasure but worthy of the time shared.

Then there was a happy pause at a sprawling, forested park one other day. We bought some chicken nuggets with a soft drink and sat in the car under huge oak trees without a sound to be heard, save only for the tweets of a few robins.

We've both felt more "retired" up here. We seem to have less to do, less to concern ourselves with, accepting our doctor's orders and adhering to our diets. But what caused us to feel differently in Florida? Maybe because we always had something to accomplish, some deadline to reach.

We think the cause was the excess population when the snowbirds and tourists flew in. It caused more hard work just to avoid traffic accidents. And the fact that so many additional people occupied the same space as in the off-season was a factor. To secure a comfortable seat in a favorite restaurant meant you had to arrive earlier and compete for a table. And that risked ruining lunch over stress.

So the reality of reducing the stresses in our life provided a much more comfortable lifestyle. And that resulted in fewer aches and pains and more restful sleep, both welcome additions to our life.

As I've said before about the weather . . . it's been wonderful so far in St. Louis. But I can't say the same for Fort Myers. It's gotten pretty hot for this early in the year (low-nineties on June 2nd) and folks are bracing for a mighty hot one, along with the normal amount of Hurricanes for the summer.

Speaking of hurricanes. Early in our tenure down there, on August 9th of 2004, we encountered Hurricane Charley, quite a bad one with winds reaching almost 150 miles an hour. On the invitation of our pastor, we joined him and a few other friends in our Parish Church.

We rode it out in there, discovering later that it was quite possibly the worst place to be. The building had a high vaulted ceiling and, thank the Lord, it *did* hold up. But it was an experience we didn't enjoy. We didn't receive much damage to our house but it was humanly frightening.

On August 30th, in 2017, we had another serious Hurricane pass through our neighborhood. Irma was her name and she reached 177 miles per hour. For that one, we were forced to evacuate and found overnight housing in a local Hotel. The Hurricane passed over our heads through the night with very damaging winds. The Hotel had no electricity and the CNN television network broadcast from the main lobby as we watched them use an auxiliary power source.

We drove home to examine our house the next morning after the winds quieted and we surveyed major damage to our trees and landscaping. But the house itself stood firm.

Interestingly, we had two cats at the time and we took them to the hotel with us. They remained under the bed all night and unwillingly crawled out with the sunrise.

What followed with our return home were six days and nights without air conditioning and temps in the mid-nineties. Ginny swore that it would be the last Hurricane she ever experienced. It was.

It's no secret that riding out a Hurricane is a scary experience, a bad one, and not something I enjoy recalling. Enough about hurricanes.

CHAPTER TWENTY-ONE

Wrapping It Up

As I prepare to end this written endeavor, I am obligated to explain our financial situation. It's important as a point of reference and if for no other reason, to satisfy your curiosity. It also might shed a bit more light on the incentives for our actions.

First of all, we are not millionaires. Never were, never will be. We differed from most of our neighbors and friends in that respect but it never troubled us and certainly didn't bother them. They could assume from the cars we drove and our conservative spending habits that we didn't have a lot to burn at the end of each month.

But as time went on and our house aged, we were beginning to run dangerously low in our proverbial "nest-egg." We had underestimated the cost to maintain a 20- year-old house and our monthly budgeting was putting us behind in our projections for the future.

The greatest underestimation was in the area of life-expectancy. Here we were in our mid-eighties and still relatively healthy. Problem was, we shouldn't have been. We weren't going to have enough to live on for the rest of our lives if we lived much longer. By any account, we should've died a long time ago and we wouldn't have had the same financial issues. But it wasn't reasonable to be unhappy about being healthy. Or was it?

It was clear. Something had to give. The move "To be with our kids up north," had a secondary purpose. Since we were living over our heads, there wouldn't be enough money to maintain the house for much longer. We were being forced to *downsize* regardless of where we lived. Even if we remained in Fort Myers, we were destined to move into a rental and sell the house.

All of that explains why it's imperative to sell now, sooner rather than later. We're not starving, nor are we running out of money, but we can't afford to maintain two separate dwellings for much longer. We can do it *somewhat* longer, but not indefinitely.

Nothing much we can do about any of that. Except pray, listen closely to the advice of our realtor (and our God), both on about the same level right now, and spend a bit of money to patch up some things that need attention on the house. That's it. The results are in the hands of Almighty God.

Here's a local *slip* right now that's appropriate. I've mentioned before that we have a small *balcony* on the back side of our current apartment. Most would call it a *patio* but because it's above the ground and is an extension of the building itself, ownership refers to it as a *balcony*. Because of the elevation of the building and the ground, it's supported by large wooden beams on one side and resembles what many might call a *deck*.

At any rate, this spot has become a great place for me to meditate, relax, and to reflect . . . alone. I'm out there every afternoon around 5:00pm, calling it my "happy hour" because I enjoy a beer and a small snack. I'll be in for supper promptly at 6:00. It's an hour segment of each day that I personally anticipate and value. Not that I want to separate from Ginny, but because we both use that time to resolve either family or personal issues in our own mind.

I've got to further describe my *balcony*. It extends from sliding doors about six feet outward from the house and covers about a dozen feet in distance along the side of the building. It's about 100+ square feet, large enough for two chairs, a few flowering plants, and a small table.

Now, it's the surrounding area that sets the balcony apart from most in the complex. It's lined with tall and beautiful trees that rise up at least 200 feet and are home to dozens of birds and squirrels. They keep the treetops trimmed and animated.

And oh, there are sounds, too. Sounds of breaking branches, falling leaves, and an array of songs from the variety of birds. Because of the architecture, the balcony sits halfway up the trees. So I'm sitting in what resembles a tree house in the midst of these towering natural structures.

I can't say enough for the value of this small piece of property. It's replaced my back porch in Florida and does the job quite well, providing a quiet place to reason and resolve problems.

Add to this the occasional good fortune of having a son stop by for conversation, and I'm in heaven. It's never an interruption to see a family visitor. It keeps us close and reminds me of that important reason we're back here in the first place. For any visitor, it's my opportunity to receive counsel that isn't requested but never refused.

Another quiet place in which to escape, my *office*. That's a loose interpretation of the word "office" since it's really a guest bedroom. But because of the scarcity of space, I have a small desk and computer in that room and use it for writing stuff like this. It's plenty large for doing that and if a guest ever needs it, I'm out of here.

Must tell you about a wonderful evening Ginny and I enjoyed last night. We took one of our sons to dinner to say "Thank you" for all the special help he gave us during the move-in.

We went to an elegant Italian restaurant in our neighborhood and noticed as we entered that the skies were becoming unusually dark. As we began eating, the place rocked with the sound and the flashing lights of a severe thunderstorm. We could follow it across the horizon through a window and also throughout the restaurant as the lightning illuminated the entire place. It was very noisy.

But just as we finished our dinners and walked to the front door, the sky had changed to more friendly colors. And around the sprawling clouds, we gazed at the beauty of a magnificent double rainbow. Its vivid colors shone through a complete arc from left to right. It was one of the clearest rainbows we had ever seen as it lit our way home to the front door, a dramatic end to the evening.

We noticed during the dinner, as we had come to notice whenever we were with our kids, they also shared our unusual happiness. They knew these were precious days they never would have had if we remained in Florida. From time to time, they verbalized their added peace and their gratitude for our making the move. Of course, it wasn't necessary but it sure did mean a lot to two old parents who felt they had done the right thing.

Since we enjoyed more visits together as a family these days, we explained that our plans for the future included burial in a cemetery near our apartment that belonged to our original Parish, St. Joseph's. We purchased the plots and were happy to see the destination we considered our ultimate "Home" in our book, *Grace Will Lead Us Home.*

There was also St. Agnes Retirement Home nearby, a truly remarkable residence. Ginny and I visited there recently, appraised the living choices, and walked the beautiful grounds. If we were ever to be separated by God's will, St. Agnes would be a pleasant home where the surviving spouse could find excellent care and contentment.

Being in St. Louis to personally explain those many things about our future, gave both Ginny and I great peace and comfort. And also, having the kids nearby for emergencies, was also comforting.

On a more positive note, this morning's paper featured a story that suggested a future trip and overnight visit. The headline read: *"You Never Sausage a Place."* And that pretty much told the story of the Hermann Missouri Wurst Haus.

The charming red brick building on the Missouri River town's historic First Street has grown in eight years from a simple German deli with 18 seats to a restaurant with 90 seats and cases of homemade meats including a large variety of smoked sausages with cranberry and hot pepper cheese, German bologna, best of show Bratwurst from a basic recipe of pork and seasoning spices with a hint of onion and garlic.

Other tantalizing choices are a sausage with Caramelized Pear and Gorgonzola Cheese Bratwurst and another Brat called Bourbon Pepper Bacon. Maybe it's revealing a little too much about our country background, but any and all of these sausages are tempting enough to lure us into Hermann. Did I forget that they make their own wines and beers to accompany the lunches and dinners and/or to take back home?

I'm sure we'll enjoy every minute of many adventures into the wine country of Missouri. It's historic places like Hermann that are attractive and enticing destinations extremely different from anything in Florida. After those nearly 20 years in a desert, we're curious to learn about this other side of America with a dramatic early history all its own.

CHAPTER TWENTY- TWO

Along Came Rachael

In just a few days, our one-and-only daughter, Mary, will visit St. Louis from Ohio. She and her family live in a little town called Orville, the International Headquarters of *Smucker's*. The only unhappiness they share is living 500 miles away.

I say *unhappiness* because Mary, her husband, Tim, and their two boys named Jesse, 18, and Peter, 16, really do love and appreciate St. Louis. In their early childhood, they lived here as Dad worked for the historic, locally-born Purina.

Those were good years for strong Cardinal's teams and everyone supported them. So they'll all be visiting us for about five days and we intend to revisit some very good times, perhaps even a Cardinals game.

Shortly after *they* leave, our son, Frank, and his wife, Robin, with twin 8-year-year-old children will be visiting us from Savannah, Georgia. We assume that all of these family visitors will be sharing our two swimming pools and enjoying meals at our table and in our favorite restaurants. It will surely be a jolly time. Normally, we'd be lucky to see those people, maybe once a year. Now, we'll establish a precedent that allows for more frequent visits.

Right now, the weather is gorgeous for visitors, except at ground level. Flooding has inundated the rural areas around St. Louis and all throughout the central and northern parts of the State. The swollen Mississippi River continues to ravage the Midwest. Water levels along the river have approached records set during the Great Flood of 1993, one of the worst in American history. The flooding is expected to continue for many weeks.

Farmers have been particularly hard-hit, losing hundreds of thousands of fine, fertile acreage to the continually rising waters. It's a disaster by any one's definition with the losses soaring into multiple millions of dollars. No relief is in sight.

The flooding is setting all kinds of records for high water, even in downtown St. Louis along the riverfront. And that kind of bad news affects tourism, one of the livelihoods of the area.

The pity is, a natural disaster of this magnitude is unstoppable. Only nature can heal the wounds of months of too much water. And that takes a lot of hard work, patience, time, and God's compassion.

For many people, their high spirits and positive attitudes have been pushed to the limits. So they turn to prayer. It's all that's left in their recovery repertoire. But will it be enough to stop the rains? God did it once. The people in these parts believe He'll do it again. and He'll manifest His truth by disproving that, "You can't go home again."

And all Missourians, including newcomers like us, will fully appreciate the denouement of our story. But before that happens, Ginny and I must sell the Florida house, the Blues must win the Stanley Cup, and the flooding waters must start to recede. Is that asking too much? We'll wait and see.

By the way, over a brief pause in our activities, Ginny and I visited an excellent Family Physician recommended by a close friend. We like him very much and are particularly impressed by his bedside manner. He's in his mid-sixties, kind and compassionate, and most important, he's a good listener in answer to his detailed questions. Finding him was an important part of our puzzle. He's adjusted our levels of anxiety and peace.

So, we're taking our goals one at a time. In order of occurrence: the St. Louis Blues won the *Stanley Cup Championship* last night. For the first time in their 50+ year history. They've proved beyond a doubt that they're the best team in the National Hockey League.

The city is going absolutely crazy with plans for a parade, celebrations all over town, and would you believe, fireworks at every corner of the city and county after they won it all at 10:00pm, June 12th. It's great to be part of such an achievement. Lots of good people waited very long for this time and they're showing their joy. We're happy to be a very small part of it. Our timing was just right for a Championship, another good sign for the Ungers.

Still another one: I was sitting out on the balcony the other evening with a friend and something caught my eye around his shoulder. I asked him if he also saw it. He exclaimed, "Yes!" And I replied that I had never seen *fireflies* this early in the summer season, in early June.

Actually, fireflies, which are a type of beetle, share a relationship with weather that goes deeper than the summer solstice. Their larvae live under the ground during winter, mature during spring, and then emerge in early summer anywhere from the third week in May to the third week in June. So they were right on time for Missouri but I learned the hard way that Southwest Florida was not a common place for them to be found.

At first, we spotted just one tiny, blinking light pulsating beautifully against green trees as the sky darkened and the sun set. In just a matter of minutes the air around us was illuminated like the *Magic Kingdom*, nearly bringing tears to my eyes. I hadn't seen those critters for over twenty years and it was a mere introduction of Summer joys to come.

Then, just a day later, three of our children came together with their families to honor their dad for Father's Day in our new family epicenter of St. Louis. What a wonderful time we had. The happiest part for me was seeing the joy in Ginny's eyes. It was truly an answer to her dreams to sit in a room again surrounded by several of her children. Her smile was absolutely priceless.

That single scene made the entire *Moving Experience* worth the while. The sacrifices and challenges had undergone a transformation into laughter, joking and congeniality. There were already plans on the table for getting all of our children from around the country to join at Christmas in our new location. That will most certainly be the crème de la crème for closing a year of multiple miracles for all of us.

Speaking of miracles, just today, June 20th 2019, the headlines on our Post Dispatch newspaper read, "FLOODWATERS RECEDE." That was enough for us. It established the second requirement for ending this book, the end of the floods.

When I read the official report, it was the wonderful news that everyone was waiting to hear, especially the hundreds of growers who were so seriously deprived of their income. They still have a long way to go but the beginning of the end has arrived, the floodwaters are down. So my story is near completion. But then, along came Rachael!

You'll recall that Ginny and I have a special child named John who is mentally different. He's 62 years old and has the mentality of a 2-year old. And yet he is lovable, handsome, and, indeed, special, all in a very unusual way. John does not and cannot communicate in any manner. And we, all the members of his family, both at his Special School and at home, have missed that act of sharing.

But this morning, I received a unique reward from another very special person. Her name was Rachael. I had never met her before.

It happened in a Donut Shop near our house appropriately called *The Donut Palace.* I visit there almost every day and force myself to limit my consumption of luscious sweets to one per day, with a cup of coffee to help the sugar go down.

On this morning, I selected a table facing a large window that allowed me to watch comers and goers in the parking lot. Well, I happened to see a young girl, maybe 14 or 15 years old accompanied by her father. She was physically beautiful in a special way with a broad, broad smile and long, naturally-curly hair.

As they entered, I heard her father say, "Rachael, which one would you like?" She pointed silently to a favorite donut and the server removed two from the case and placed them into a bag. During the process, this lovely effeminate creature, walked over to my table and without hesitation looked into my eyes and said in a friendly tone, "I saw you through the window when I walked by."

I melted, holding back tears. She was so sincere. I looked up at her and returned her smile with an equally friendly, "Well, hello. I saw you, too. Do you like this place?" Rachael nodded in the affirmative as I said, "I like this place, too. I come here all the time to eat donuts."

And that was it. Her father beckoned for her to join him as he walked out the door. Rachael smiled at me one more time as she faded away into the car and drove off with her dad.

Neither one of those people will ever know how I was moved by that beautiful conversation, one that lasted, maybe, ten seconds. But it *made* the rest of my day, and week and month and year. For Rachael was like our son, John, a very special child with a very large smile.

I thought of John and how we would love to communicate with him in such a simple manner. But for the time being, Rachael's kindness and big smile had to satisfy our need for *positive* influence.

Case in point: we recently celebrated John's 61st birthday at his home, with his four roommates joining us. Truly, it was not a celebration, becoming yet another painful experience for Ginny and me, another one that will never go away, for all the wrong reasons.

At the beginning, things went okay because we showed him a gift-bag filled with things he really likes, e.g., cookies, magazines, an outrageous hat and sunglasses that he loves dearly. (Of course, he always looks silly in that garb, but it makes him smile and his roommates smile with him.)

But then we walked into his bedroom with walls and windows he decorates with colorful objects. He loves that, too, pressing small plastic forms and shapes against the flat surfaces. They joined his most treasured objects, a collection of stuffed animals on his dresser.

The most significant gift we brought him was *another* stuffed animal, a dog that was large enough to frighten him and cause him to demonstrate his dislike with loud screams. When he does that, it is frightening to anyone within earshot.

He shouts at the top of his lungs, sending high-level screams throughout the home and scaring those around him, including his parents.

Ginny and I quickly removed the dog and John gradually returned to normal. We understood his behavior, feeling sad at his inability to comprehend that the stuffed dog was harmless.

As a matter of fact, John never did care much for dogs because they jumped on him and barked loudly. That frightened him. And since he could not comprehend language, he complained in the only way he knew, with loud screams of fear and a threatening flail of his arms.

After an hour of visiting, Ginny and I hugged and kissed John and once again left him behind. We held one another and wiped tears from our eyes. I shared some deep feelings as she agreed that she had felt the same. I explained that many times, I feel such deep pain and sorrow in my heart that I experience a physical shudder, a kind of shortness of breath that in many cases actually frightens me.

This led us to shed even more tears over a lunch of healing. But we would be okay, as long as we had each other to share the sadness of a son named John.

Once again, we marveled at the blessing that God had given us in confirming that St. Louis *is* the right place for us. If we had remained in Florida, we never would have been touched in quite the same way by the special angel named *Rachael* nor the other special angel named *John.*

There is a *Psalm* written in the Old Testament of the Bible that promises: "Those who sow in tears will reap in songs of joy." That is our infinite hope.

On another note: I came across an obituary the other day that really hit home. After reading all you have up until now, you'll immediately see why it was of such great interest to Ginny and me.

First of all, a man who passed away had written his own obit. During the last year of his life, he had left Florida and moved back to St. Louis into an independent assistant living retirement community. The reason for his move was that he wanted to be reunited with his biological family and make peace with those he loved most. (Sound familiar?)

The obit then listed, as is customary, those he left behind; e.g., children, grandchildren, and many other important people, like those who cared for him the last years of his life. It ended with, "He will be remembered by many for his generous nature and for being a philanthropist on a personal level."

The irony of his story left a lump in our throats and a clear understanding of his motivation for doing what he did. (His name is omitted to honor his privacy.) The man's story was our personal discovery with absolute proof that we weren't the first, nor the last, to have relocated for loved ones.

On a far less serious topic of a totally different nature, I enjoyed a pleasurable experience the other night on my balcony. This one wasn't as significant as those final stories, but it did touch a nerve.

While I'm sitting there enjoying the silence of the moment, flanked by towering trees and a radiant sunset, a unique sound stole my attention. In an instant, I was overwhelmed by a crescendo of noise from the woods behind me. It was the indigenous Missouri *cicada* who was in its 17-year periodic emergence from hibernation.

What a deafening sound it was, a symphonic mating ritual made by both sexes. The music can be sweet to some, annoying to others. Its caused by elastic membranes behind the last pair of legs on the tiny creature. The result of rubbing makes a loud clicking noise that eventually becomes an audible nuisance if one allows it.

Notably, the insects dig their way from underneath to above the ground where they cover hundreds of acres for a period of a few weeks. After shedding their outsides, the insects leave for another seventeen years, unless their cousins, the *annual* cicadas show up during the same time period. They all somehow manage to avoid each other as they dig themselves back into the soil.

Experts claim that the creatures aren't unique to Missouri but they're not observed anywhere near our previous home in the state of Florida, another "something" we never would have experienced if we remained in that location.

And so, with that inconsequential news, I seal this book (almost) and move on to another experience, hopefully, not another *Moving* one like this. But I thank you for moving *with* Ginny and me and sharing our ups and downs to reach this upper in an amazing new life. Ginny has a little plaque hung in our kitchen that reads, "Love lives here!" And it does. We learned that lesson more than anything else over these past months.

It's been a long ride, one loaded with failures and achievements, disappointments and joys. We've experienced so many new things, even at the ages of 83 and 84. We had many doubts along the way, doubts, fears and tears. But in the end, if our journey strikes you as *encouraging*, then make a move yourself some day, bolstered by the faith, hope, love and support of your family.

And remember, those climate changes aren't reserved exclusively for south/north moves. They also run from east to west and the other way, too. To be sure, the little choices along the way are usually filled with suspense, success and surprise.

I wouldn't dare call Ginny and me superheroes for surviving all of this. We simply elected to continue learning as we made these the most exciting years of our lives. Further, we don't want our story to close until God says it's okay . . .

AND HE JUST DID!

AMAZING GRACE
John Newton, English Poet, 1779

Amazing grace! How sweet the sound
That saved a wretch like me!
I once was lost, but now am found;
Was blind, but now I see.
'Twas grace that taught my heart to fear,
And grace my fears relieved;
How precious did that grace appear
The hour I first believed.
Through many dangers, toils, and snares,
I have already come;
'Tis grace hath brought me safe thus far,
And grace will lead me home.
The Lord has promised good to me,
His Word my hope secures;
He will my Shield and Portion be,
As long as life endures.
Yea, when this flesh and heart shall fail,
And mortal life shall cease,
I shall possess, within the veil,
A life of joy and peace.
The earth shall soon dissolve like snow,
The sun forbear to shine;
But God, who called me here below,
Will be forever mine.
When we've been there ten thousand years,
Bright shining as the sun,
We've no less days to sing God's praise
Than when we'd first begun.